I0648178

*Psychiatry* and the Bible

# *Psychiatry*
# and the Bible

CARROLL A. WISE

HARPER & BROTHERS: *New York*

PSYCHIATRY AND THE BIBLE

Copyright © 1956, by Harper & Brothers
Printed in the United States of America

All rights in this book are reserved.
No part of the book may be used or reproduced
in any manner whatsoever without written per-
mission except in the case of brief quotations
embodied in critical articles and reviews. For
information address Harper & Brothers
49 East 33rd Street, New York 16, N. Y.

Library of Congress catalog card number: 56–7025

258
W812p

48953

TO MY FATHER
and to the
Memory of my Mother

# CONTENTS

# INTRODUCTION

THIS book had its origin in the conviction that the problems of religion and health could be interpreted through the medium of the Bible. Today there is a strong interest in the relation of religion to illness and health. Many are looking for the answers to problems of daily living, such as anxiety. There is also strong interest in the Bible and Biblical studies. The Bible, being a record of man's search for the meaning of human experience, is as contemporary as though it were written yesterday. It presents man in the perspective of a God who is like the central figure of the Bible, Christ. While there is validity in a point of view which sees man as man, the Christian faith holds that man and his problems cannot be fully understood unless also seen in the light of the creative, loving God who is seeking his redemption. It is this perspective which the Bible furnishes as does no other book.

In pastoral counseling many persons are seen who are looking for easy solutions to life problems. The idea is widespread that man's mind is something of a machine which can be adjusted by easy reassurance. The appeal of this approach is that it relieves the individual of the responsibility of facing and dealing with painful elements of his experience. It promises a great deal in return for very little and ends in disillusionment.

This is not, therefore, an attempt to write another self-help book. Long ago we learned that we are hurt by persons and we are cured through persons. No book will cure serious life problems, for life is not a series of mathematical equations, nor the working out of a definite formula, scientific or otherwise. It is a constant process of relationships between ourselves and our world, other persons and God, through which conditions are being created in us and in others that we have learned to call illness or health. Therefore, any cure or solution of our problems must take place in and through these relationships. The deeper, dynamic aspects of personality and interpersonal relations cannot be radically changed by conscious ideas forced down from the outside, but only through living relationships which are of a nature that makes growth possible from within.

My aim therefore is to write in a way which will help the reader to understand something of himself and his experience. To the extent that self-understanding is part of any real cure or solution, I hope this book will have a positive influence. But many times it will simply point the direction in which a cure or solution may be found. The actual finding of answers will have to be through relationships with another person who is qualified in heart and mind to give necessary help.

Further, my aim is to bring understanding through the method of relating the insights of modern medicine and psychiatry to those of religious faith as expressed in the Bible. Some students of these two fields, psychiatry and religion, have been impressed with the fact that they wrestle with many common problems. Others have emphasized the conflicts. Here we are concerned with their positive relationships. Not that we can identify psychiatry with religion. They are not the same and should not be forced into any common mold. But the insights which they bring to the problems of life should be looked at together and be understood in the light shed by each. To the extent that any science throws light on human life it is not foreign to the spirit of the Christian faith which seeks the truth leading to freedom.

This book is written so that it may be read as any book is read, or so that it can be used by groups in study. Some of the material is similar to articles that have appeared in the Methodist Church School quarterly, *The Adult Student*, but it has been completely revised and rewritten. In order to facilitate its use in discussion groups and personal study we have quoted the Biblical text freely; we have made references to all Biblical material used and have suggested passages for study; and we have suggested reading for those who wish to go further. It is our hope that the book may serve as a basis for both youth and adult discussion groups.

It is impossible to acknowledge everyone to whom the author is indebted, for they are legion. It was Professor Rollin H. Walker of Ohio Wesleyan who first opened the profound insights and resources of the Scriptures, but other teachers and colleagues have added to this beginning. It was Dr. Anton T. Boisen, father of the clinical pastoral training movement, who first opened the rich source of insights into religious experience to be found in the study of the disturbed mind. He and those who have been my colleagues in the Council for Clinical Training through the years have contributed greatly to my growth. My relationships with physicians, psychiatrists and other students in the field of health and illness have been many and rich. From many authors I have drawn insights to which direct acknowledgment has not been given, but for which gratitude is felt. Students and persons who have come for counseling have raised many questions and have been the source of insight. The text has been read by several colleagues on the Garrett faculty, Dr. Ernest Saunders, Professor of New Testament Interpretation, and Dr. Otto Baab, Professor of Old Tesament Interpretation, and by Dr. Carl Christensen, a psychiatrist. I am grateful for the many helpful suggestions and encouragement given by each of these men. Gratitude and appreciation is deeply felt toward my family who have eased legitimate demands that time might be available to write. Appreciation is also due to Mrs. Billie Brown, who very graciously handled the secretarial work.

CARROLL A. WISE

*Psychiatry* and the Bible

## Chapter One

# Health, Religion
# and the Whole Man

MAN cannot get away from his body. His life is lived in and through it. It gives joy and pain. Through it he achieves superb victories over various aspects of existence, and through it he commits hideous crimes. He experiences his body in illness and in health and finds it a handicap to, or a channel for, the release of energy. His body has the power of procreation, as is true of all living organisms. In some ways it seems simple and understandable, in other ways it is exceedingly complex and intricate. Eventually it is cast off as an old garment which is no longer capable of clothing the human spirit or of being a continuing medium for its expression.

Man cannot get away from his mind, either. He thinks and tries to find meaning in his experience and ponders many questions about himself and life. He knows many feelings, painful and pleasurable—fear, anxiety, hate, guilt, love, faith, hope, courage. He feels emotional hungers and experiences frustration or satisfaction. He knows the heights of emotional joy or the depths of despair. He is capable of a profound sense of worth, or an equally profound sense of worthlessness. Through his imagination he may create a new world for himself or destroy the one he now inhabits. But he cannot get away from himself. His body is part of the self, and affects the self, and the self has a profound effect on the body.

Neither can man get away from other persons. He is born into a family, is raised by them or by foster parents, has brothers and sisters, friends, teachers, physicians, policemen, business associates, pastors and a host of other acquaintances. With all of them he develops relationships, and for better or worse these relationships affect both him and the others. Early relationships are known to be the most powerful in determining the direction of his personality development. Out of his relationships with other persons come feelings and ideas which influence the health of his mind and of his body. His relationships with others are fraught with great potentialities for either good or evil, but he cannot get away from them.

Furthermore, man cannot get away from God. He may think he can, he may try and even think he succeeds; he may substitute other words for "God," but he cannot escape from the fundamental reality that creates, undergirds, and sustains all of life. In his fear he may turn and run only to be swallowed up by the very fear by which he is being driven; in his rebellion he may assert his omnipotence and supremacy and project himself into the place of God, only to find himself defeated by his own rebellion; or in love he may respond with an attitude of trust through which he feels a deep sense of kinship with the Ultimate Source of his being. If he pierces through the demands made on him by other persons to the demands which are rooted in the very nature of life itself and to which no man can add or subtract—if he gains such insight he will discover a moral order in life as certain as the natural order which science reveals. God as an old man up in the sky—intelligent persons got away from that idea of God long ago, though many fearful persons still cling to it. But God in the sense of the Ultimate Reality who creates and sustains life—no man can get away from that. In man's most profound moods he still asks,

> Whither shall I go from thy Spirit?
> Or whither shall I flee from thy presence?[1]

In each of these aspects of man's being he can become sick. Physical sickness due to the invasion of disease germs is familiar to all of us, and illustrates how our environment may make us ill. One may also be sick in his relation to himself, as in the person who constantly feels guilty about his need for love. Or one may have a sick relationship with others, an illustration of which is the fear that stimulates constant withdrawal from them. Or a person's relation with God may be sick, as illustrated by the one who constantly feels that God is condemning him. As a matter of fact, a man who is sick in one of these relationships is likely to be sick in all of them. No matter where the origin may be when a person becomes ill in one area his total personality is likely to suffer. By sickness we mean a condition in which an individual cannot function as he was meant to function; in which his energies are consumed in a destructive struggle rather than being freed for creative, positive experiences.

It is becoming clearer through the study of sick people why, throughout the centuries, man has found religious questions growing out of the experience of illness. Illness brings us face to face with certain basic issues. What is the meaning of life? What is the nature and purpose of life which involves physical, emotional or spiritual suffering? If this illness ends my life, then what? Does all emotional or spiritual suffering, for example, all anxiety, always have to lead to illness? Or can one learn how to endure some suffering without becoming ill? What does it mean to learn to overcome or endure suffering? Questions raised by the book of Job are still questions that trouble thoughtful people as they face the meaning of their own experiences of suffering.

Many people in the state of good health never permit themselves to think of these issues but in a state of serious illness they quickly experience what has been called "the anxiety of fate and death." It is doubtful if any thinking man can be completely and continually oblivious to the question of his own destiny, or fully accept the fact of his own death.

The experience of illness brings us face to face with the unknown, and the unknown is always a source of anxiety. To be sure, medical science has done and is doing a great deal to bring the unknown causes of many illnesses into the realm of knowledge and in this way to learn to control or cure the illness. However, we are still a long way from anything that could be called a complete mastery of illness. Such a condition would indeed be a state of Utopia which would border on the fantastic.

In our anxiety about illness, we ask the doctor, "What do I have; how did I get it; and what is the cure?" But as we talk with our pastor, we are likely to ask, "What did I do to deserve this; for what am I being punished; what is the meaning of this experience in terms of my life and ultimate destiny?" Science may succeed in pushing back the horizons of the unknown in terms of factual cause and effect relationships in illness, but science will never succeed in breaking through the horizons of the unknown in terms of meaning and destiny of individual life. This is beyond science.

There is another aspect of an experience of illness which creates anxiety, bringing to awareness the impotency of our conscious will to overcome such experiences. This limitation is freely recognized in certain types of illnesses, but not in others. We do not expect a man whose illness takes a physical form to cure himself by an act of will. However, we are more inclined to expect a person whose illness takes the form of abnormal mental or behavior symptoms to use his will to effect a cure. Thus it is held that the alcoholic ought to have enough will power to abstain from drinking, and the one who has undue anxiety about some minor event ought to have enough will power to control his anxiety.

When we take a more realistic view of our illness, we discover that cure lies in quite a different direction than calling on our will. First, we have to discover the conditions out of which the illness arose. Next, we have to find ways to reverse those conditions and their effect on the body or mind or on our total being. Then we have to discover ways of continuing to live so that the conditions creating illness are not repeated. This idea of discovering the conditions of illness and of the cure of illness is much more easily accepted by the average person in regard to physical illnesses than in regard to emotional and spiritual illnesses. In these latter experiences many still feel that they ought to be able to manipulate themselves out of their symptoms without dealing radically with the conditions out of which the illness grows. And sometimes this idea is preached to them by the church.

√As modern science has progressed in its understanding of the conditions which create illness, it has come to insights which are very closely akin to the insights of the Bible. The Bible emphasizes the fundamental relationship which man has to himself, to others and to God. Insights recorded in the Bible have come through what religion calls revelation; that is, the act through which God reveals his own nature and the nature of man. On the human side, revelation is received through the intuitive processes guided by faith. Scientific views of illness have come through a different approach; that is, through the study of many incidences of illness and an attempt to discover the common meaning of these experiences. Starting at opposite ends with diverse methods, Biblical insights and medical insights today have a great deal in common. It is for this reason that an attempt is made to relate the insights of modern psychiatry and modern medicine to the insights of religion as they are found in the Bible. And we shall see that both the religious and scientific approaches have a unique contribution to make, neither of which can be made by the other.

√ Now illness as an experience needs to be distinguished from the concept of a disease. A disease is a process that takes place within an organism. Tuberculosis is an illustration of a disease. But illness is always the experience of a person, involving the individual's feelings and attitudes toward the disease which is present within him and his consequent reactions. It involves the way in which he seeks, consciously or unconsciously, to use the disease for the solution of a problem. In many situations, the doctor realizes that he not only needs to know what the disease is, but he needs to know the kind of person in whom he finds the disease, and the surroundings in which the person lives. The attitudes and feelings of the person may be crucial to the cure of the disease, as may be the attitudes and feelings of his family and others. Religion may have little or nothing to say about a given disease, but it has a great deal to say about the person who has the disease, and the quality of his relationships to others and to God. The person, therefore, is the center around which the experiences and interest of religion in relation to illness and health revolve. Religion is interested in the person as a bearer of an ultimate destiny and is therefore concerned with immediate experiences which are either a threat to, or impetus toward, that destiny. Medicine deals more directly with the disease process than does religion; the function of religion is to enable persons to find inner resources which give strength in the encounter with the disease process. This strength may or may not contribute to cure.

There is another way of coming to understand the meaning of illness and health. In illness, one part of the organism is controlling the whole man. This part may be a particular organ; it may be a strong feeling; or it may be a disturbing relationship. Because a part is controlling the whole, the individual cannot function as he was meant to function. Health is a condition in which each part is furthering its particular purpose in relation to the whole organism; each part is contributing to the welfare of the whole. Furthermore, each part is integrated and unified by the whole being. In other words, health is wholeness.

Health is also fulfillment, meaning the fulfillment of the function or purpose of each part of the organism, not only the physical parts, but the emotional, intellectual, social and religious aspects of the personality. We quickly recognize that if the body of a child does not grow according to its inherent possibilities, the child becomes sick. The same thing is true of the emotional life of the individual. Many become ill because of conditions or relationships which prevent adequate and proper emotional development. If we cannot grow in our capacity for love, for example, we will become ill. This block in growth may be due to faulty relationships with certain people and in turn may develop further unhealthy relationships. When this is the case, usually our relationship to God is also unhealthy. The expression and development of the potentialities within us is an essential element of wholeness and of health.

The fact leads us to a basic idea of man as an organism in which the body and the mind are but different aspects of one total being. This organism lives within an environment which acts on it and to which it reacts. So close is this relationship between the organism and its environment that one scientist, J. S. Haldane, has said that "the organism is one with its environment," suggesting a kind of unity or integration in fundamental relationships within the organism and between the organism and its environment that is both very subtle and very powerful. Beyond this relationship there is the recognition that there is no purely physical illness nor mental illness, but that all illness is an experience of the whole person, whether the symptoms happen to be on the organic level or on the level of the mind. This close relationship between the organism and its environment is of special interest to religion, since religion, at least as the Christian faith sees it, is basically a matter of man's relationship to God, to himself and to his fellow men.

The idea of the causes of illness needs some clarification. Ordinarily we think of an illness as having a single cause which operates rather mechanically to produce its effect. But a deeper view of human experience shows that this idea excludes important facts.

An illness may have a causative factor such as the tubercle bacilli in tuberculosis. But this is not necessarily the cause of the illness. Not all persons in whom such bacilli are present become ill. There are within each organism forces which tend to ward off bacilli and make the organism immune. There are also other forces which tend to make the organism hospitable to the bacilli. One formulation of such forces is found in the phrases, "the will to recover," or "the will to be sick," or "the will to die." These forces are to be understood in the sense of feelings and desires which may stimulate the organism in one or other of these directions. Illness and health, rather than being the result of a single mechanical cause, are the result of complicated forces constantly at work within the person and between the person and his world.

What is true of any one of us in this respect is true of all of us. It is therefore true of our relationships with one another. In these relationships forces working toward health will find expression and development; likewise forces working toward illness. In some relationships healthy forces are predominant; in others, unhealthy. Each of us, for example, makes demands on others; others make demands on us. Some can accept and satisfy these demands; others cannot. Certain demands are excessive and are difficult for anyone to satisfy and remain healthy. Anxieties in one will tend to foster anxieties in others who are not stronger; trust in one will tend to foster trust in others. Our existence is lived in a continuous give and take in which life-building or life-destructive forces are being knowingly and unknowingly released. For better or worse each of us is part and parcel of this tremendous process and, for the most part, we are not aware of our involvement.

But there is another side to this reciprocal relationship. Each organism has some capacity to determine its own unique response to the conditions which life presents. Even the infant is not to be thought of as a blotter that absorbs or a mirror which reflects its environment. As is frequently remarked by parents, the infant has a mind of its own. In other words it responds in a spontaneous way, determined by factors within itself. It is exercising a potentiality which sometimes is called autonomy and sometimes called freedom; a response-ability of the organism.

This spontaneity or autonomy leads to the question of responsibility, not in terms of blame, but in terms of being willing to use or learn how to use the positive forces of life. Responsibility utilizes the capacity to feel what one requires of life as well as what life requires of one and to make those decisions or choices which are necessary for fulfillment. The person who refuses (as many do out of fear) to exercise his freedom and to learn to respond or make choices in ways that contribute to health will become sick and remain sick. Health often lies in the direction of becoming aware of the life-growing and life-destroying forces in oneself and in one's relationships with others, and in being able and willing to make those decisions or choices which throw the weight of our conscious, self-directing capacities on the creative side.

At this point, there is a danger of misunderstanding. It is not that we can decide to become healthy and presto! we are healthy. Health is not to be gained by wishing for it nor even by "working" for it directly. It is to be found by fulfilling basic conditions. Health or illness are, to a large measure, the result of the feeling responses or decisions which a person makes in many specific relationships.

For instance, in many situations we become anxious. Anxiety is a basic response which gives pain and therefore presents a problem. Anxiety in itself does not produce illness, but it may be handled in a way which leads to illness. For a person to deceive himself and say he is not anxious when he is, can be definitely unhealthy. Or to deceive himself by saying his anxiety is justified when it is not, is · likewise unhealthy. But to know why he is anxious, to evaluate the causes of his anxiety and its consequences, and to decide whether he can relinquish or resolve his anxiety, whether he will learn to control it rather than allowing it to control him—these are basic steps in the direction of health. Here the person is learning to determine his own responses. He is acting on the fact that his anxiety is his, no one's else, and only he can deal with it constructively. To expect another to solve his problem for him is to deny himself the use of his capacity to make his own decisions and choices. This is equally true whether that other be another person or God.

The willingness and ability to take responsibility for oneself and one's reactions to life is a sign of mature health. It is an ability which the child gradually learns to utilize as he develops in an atmosphere of loving support, increasing autonomy and realistic demands and expectancy. Failure to achieve this responsibility means illness of one kind or another. A neurosis, for example, is an illness in which the conscious self and its attitudes and activities are rather completely determined by forces outside the conscious control of that self. The individual's behavior is over-determined, that is, it is more determined than it should be by motives unknown to the self. The element of choice, of freedom, of decisive control has been lost from the functioning of the self. There are reasons why this loss has occurred. Usually it happens before we are old enough to have adequately developed this spontaneity and self-determination. We cannot regain this ability by consciously desiring it, but only through adequate treatment. And for some folk this basic impulse toward determining one's own responses, or responsibility, has been so crushed and underdeveloped that it is impossible to re-establish its functioning after an illness has developed.

It is easy to become confused at this point. Plainly there are conditions which determine the way in which we function and which play a dominant role in producing illness or health. It is also plain that we cannot change many of these internal or external relationships by force of will, but can only offset their effects by understanding and changing the nature of the relationships. Furthermore, we see there is something of a self-determining quality or potentiality in man, the ability to learn to control his own responses, and at crucial points to make decisions which determine the direction of his life. He also has the ability to understand the nature of his responses and decisions or to justify and reinforce them.

This leads to the question, Is man determined or free? The answer is that he is both. What each of us becomes is a direct result of the kind of relationships which we have had and continue to have with other people. It is also the result of the kind of responses which we have made in those relationships. Life is always lived in some kind of a dynamic balance between external determination and inner self-determination or it is out of balance. It cannot be put in a simple now-it-is-this, now-it-is-that formula, but both aspects are constantly operating in every interpersonal relationship. Practically it means that for health experiences such as love have to be coming to us from outside of ourselves, but also that we must be able to make a trusting and accepting response to what we receive by learning to give.

What does the Bible have to say about these experiences? Here we move from a modern scientific point of view to ancient insights grounded in religious experience. One of the differences between these points of view is that the man of science seeks to study factual data objectively, while the genuinely religious person reports insight growing out of his own inner experiences and those he is able to observe. However, there may be more of the religious in the scientific approach, and vice versa, than is usually recognized. How do these two interpretations relate to each other?

## Health and Illness in the Bible

One cannot read far in the Bible without meeting the problem of illness and health on two levels. First in specific situations, such as are presented in the book of Job or in the healing miracles of Jesus [2] in which illness is a specific problem. Second and on a deeper level, in the attempt to wrestle with the problem of the nature of man and of a life which includes illness and suffering. Illness is understood in the Bible, as are all other human experiences, in the light of a growing insight into man's relation to God and the significance of this relationship for his own experience.

In Psalm 38 there is an interesting study of a poet's interpretation of the relation of his illness to his religious life. Here the author sees his illness as the outgrowth of his sin.

> There is no soundness in my flesh
> because of thy indignation;
> there is no health in my bones
> because of my sin.

This insight is parallel to the point of view of modern psychosomatic medicine in so far as it finds one of the factors in physical illness to be intense feelings of guilt. A distinction needs to be made here between symptoms of illness being produced by feelings of guilt and the idea that illness is punishment for sin. The two ideas are closely related and may become confused. The latter implies a punishment directed from outside ourselves; the former is the result of feelings which we experience within. There is also a difference between sin and feelings of guilt. Sin is an objective condition. Feelings of guilt are subjective, and may be produced in us by conditions which are or are not our responsibility.

The mood of the writer of this Psalm is well known to the pastor who works closely with individuals or to the psychotherapist. A person may or may not put his feelings in religious terms, but physical suffering related to guilt feelings are not uncommon today. We feel in the Psalm the cry of desperation and utter distress, a sense of agony and helplessness. The poet is in the hands of a being who is punishing him as a little child might be punished by a parent.

But there is further awareness as there always is to the genuinely religious person. There is the sense that he is not suffering alone; that God knows.

> Lord, all my longing is known to thee,
>    my sighing is not hidden from thee.

Here we should keep in mind that to the ancient Hebrews knowledge was not merely intellectual knowledge as we are likely to think of it. Knowledge was always a matter of experience. God participates in this man's experience with him, so that he knows it as a fellowship of suffering rather than just knowing about it. A fuller expression of this sense of God's intimate participation in human experience is found in Psalm 139.

> O Lord, thou hast searched me and known me!
> Thou knowest when I sit down and when I rise up;
>    thou discernest my thoughts from afar.
> Thou searchest out my path and my lying down,
>    and art acquainted with all my ways.
> . . . . . . . . . . . . . . . . . . . . . . . . . . . . . . . . . . . . . . . . . . .
> Whither shall I go from thy Spirit?

Most of this Psalm is a detailed expression of the insight that man is made in the image of God and that God is constantly manifest in his experience as well as in the transcendent world. Moreover, this indwelling is not a passive relationship, but an active participation in all experience. God shares in man's experience in an active, understanding manner that makes redemption possible.

The result of this experience is not an easy removal of the symptoms. In Psalm 38 there is an expectation of God's help, but not an expression of achieved cure. There are times when religious faith operates more to make the endurance of suffering possible rather than to remove it. In this Psalm we are dealing with conflicting feelings about God. On the one side he punishes; on the other, he understands and even participates in suffering. Many people have similar conflicting feelings about God. By facing and examining such feelings we may gain insight into ourselves and into the experiences out of which these feelings grow. As we shall see later, Jesus rejected the idea that illness is punishment for sin, but enlarged on the idea that God participates with man in his suffering, seeking to turn suffering into creative experience.

Other portrayals of human experience in the book of Psalms express the same faith. In Psalm 41 God's participation in the suffering and healing process is linked to man's compassion for others. There is a suggestion here of the insight that as we have forgiven so shall we be forgiven. Compassion begets compassion. The capacity to be compassionate indicates a quality of strength in giving that in turn becomes a source of strength in receiving.

> Blessed is he who considers the poor!
> ........................................
> The Lord sustains him on his sickbed;
>     in his illness thou healest all his infirmities.

And in Psalm 103 we have the sense of God's healing work expressed in connection with a feeling of profound gratitude.

> Bless the Lord, O my soul;
> ..........................
> who forgives all your iniquity,
>     who heals all your diseases.

In some persons there is a strong tendency, after reading such passages, to picture God as something of a long-bearded physician dispensing pills out of a big black bag. They identify God with the old family doctor. This is not true to the Biblical sense of healing. For in the Bible there is a sense of a transcendent and immanent Being who is the very source of our being, One who shares suffering and joy alike, and whose healing comes through a sense of sustaining fellowship which leads us to use all of the powers which lie dormant within us for the enduring or the alleviation of ills, as the case may be.

There is another interesting use of the experience of illness in Biblical writings. It is in the tendency to diagnose social difficulties in terms of illness. Not only individuals, but groups and nations can be ill and need healing. We find an illustration of this need in Hosea 5:13–6:6. The prophet sees the nation as one who is sick and wounded and who turns to a false doctor, Assyria, who is unable to heal. He pictures God as withdrawing from the nation until it discovers its plight and is willing to repent and seek forgiveness. Like a modern surgeon, God has cut that he may heal.

> Come, let us return to the Lord;
> for he has torn, that he may heal us;
> he has stricken, and he will bind us up,
> ....................................
> that we may live before him.
> ....................................
> For I desire steadfast love and not sacrifice,
> the knowledge of God, rather
> than burnt offerings.[3]

There is a similar interpretation in Jeremiah 30:10–17. The Exile is interpreted as an incurable hurt and grievous wound for which there is no medicine nor healing. It is God's punishment for the nation's sins. In their plight, all of the nation's lovers who helped to get them into their predicament have deserted. But the prophet sees a principle of reciprocity at work; those who have devoured Israel shall be devoured and Israel's foes shall go into captivity themselves. But Israel will be healed.

> For I will restore health to you,
> and your wounds I will heal,
> says the Lord.[4]

Another reference to health on the broad social level is to be found in the book of Revelation in a description of the tree of life, "and the leaves of the tree were for the healing of the nations." [5] Here in symbolic form characteristic of the entire book of Revelation is the idea of healing taking place not only on a national scale, but for all of the nations. The Bible is so rooted in human life that it cannot avoid facing the problem of illness and health on both the personal and social levels.

When we turn to the pages of the New Testament, we find Jesus very much concerned with sick persons. Some of the accounts of healing are difficult to understand, and some seem clear on the basis of our present knowledge of the influence of emotional and spiritual factors in healing. They all have one message in common, and that is the great concern of Jesus with suffering persons. Indeed his interest seems to have been focused on the suffering person rather than on the disease itself! Also his concern was with spiritual factors such as guilt and anxiety as causes of illness, and with forgiveness and faith as necessary elements in the cure. The fact that the stories of healing in the Gospels are not complete accounts and were handed down through a number of generations by word of mouth before having been committed to writing makes precise interpretation difficult. They were never meant to be taken as exact scientific reporting, but rather to portray a message or to elaborate and illustrate an insight into the life and work of Jesus. The dangers in interpretation are either that we make far too much out of the records, unconsciously adding details and deductions out of our imagination to the story, or that we do not see in the instances cited the truth that is there.

When we try to discover the Biblical teachings in regard to illness and health we do not find a well-organized discussion leading to logical conclusions. Whatever else the Bible may be, it is not a philosophical discourse. On these issues which afflict the human spirit it has no neatly worked out answers nor easy formulas. Far from finding an intellectual explanation for suffering, its characters experience suffering and find a means of overcoming it. So Job, rejecting all of the various explanations of his friends, emerges with a victorious faith. So Jesus did not try to explain the Cross, but was able to endure it and at the same time to maintain his love toward men and his profound victorious faith in God. The Bible clearly teaches that the worst kind of illness and suffering is not to be found on the physical level, but rather is that which grows out of the isolation created when a person erects a barrier which makes it impossible for him to reach out to other persons or to God.

The understanding of the relation of religion to problems of illness and health as found in the Bible rests on the understanding of man in his relationship to God. Stated from one point of view, the

Bible is the record of God's increasing revelations of himself and his nature and consequently of the nature of his creature, man, culminating in the revelation of Christ. From another point of view, it is the record of man's increasing insight into the nature of God and into his own nature as a creature of God. These statements are not contradictory, for insight is the human side of the experience, conceived from the point of view of the divine as revelation. Unless both sides are active there is no complete experience. It is a mistake to consider man as a purely passive instrument in receiving revelation.

The kind of understanding presented in the Bible is not explanation. Explanations of illness in terms of cause and effect and specific cure have become part of God's revelation to men of science as they fulfill the conditions through which the secrets of life on this level are revealed. These conditions include persistent industrious effort, open-minded following wherever the facts may lead, and the application of reason to the problems encountered. Scientific explanations and the attendant relief and cure which they bring are of inestimable value to human life, but only a misunderstanding of both science and religion leads us to look for such explanations in the Biblical account.

Rather the Biblical account seeks to understand the nature of both man and God, and the nature of spiritual relationships out of which either illness or health may grow. The Bible always portrays man in terms much larger than any specific experience and presents specific experiences, such as illness, in this larger perspective. One way of describing this perspective is in terms of relationship, relationships between God and man, man and God and man and his fellow men.

At the outset, the Bible portrays man in the role of a creature and God in the role of the Creator.[6] This idea is not only present in the book of Genesis, but is present throughout the Scriptures. Thus the Bible presents man as organically related to an eternal Being who is the source of life. It carries one step further the insights of those scientists who see man as an organism in close reciprocal relationships to his environment, and considers both the organism which is man and the environment to which he is so closely related as originating and being sustained by the same Being.

Not only is God the Creator and man the being who is created, but God is also cast in the role of the lawgiver and man in the role of one who is free to obey or rebel against law. The story of the revelation of the nature of life, of man's relationship to God in terms of law, of man's growing insight into this law and his ability to accept and conform his life to it, is a long, dramatic, and at many points tragic, story. Some of this story is to be found in the Bible; but it has been unfolding constantly since the Biblical account closed and is finding intense expression in human life today.

Modern psychotherapy has rediscovered as its own an insight which is deep in Biblical understanding. It is that rather early in life we must learn to give up activities which aim only at the immediate satisfaction of impulses and desires, and learn to find satisfaction through long-range goals which include the welfare of others; to postpone present satisfaction so that a more mature and enriching satisfaction may be obtained later; or even to endure present suffering in order to achieve a greater joy in the future. Like Esau,[7] every man faces the alternative of selling his birthright to maturity of personality for the immediate satisfaction of less mature, childish needs. Jesus [8] faced the same issue in the temptation to make stones into bread, but chose to endure present suffering for the sake of a greater future good. These insights of the therapist are simply another way of saying that there are realities, described in terms we call law, that form the basic foundation upon which individual and social life may achieve its fullest expression and maturity. The Bible portrays these realities as rooted in the very source of our being, God.

The Bible also portrays man in another role in relation to God, that of a child or a son. "See what love the Father has given us, that we should be called children of God; and so we are." [9] "To all who received him, who believed in his name, he gave power to become children of God." [10] This concept in the New Testament is an extension and fulfillment of the idea expressed in Genesis that man is made in the image of God. In Genesis we have the suggestion of a close identity between the nature of man and the nature of God, expressed in the term "image." But it is an identity grounded more on law than on love; therefore the relationship which is essential to the complete fulfillment of identity is missing. Man is the possessor of an image without the power which makes it possible to fulfill this image, the power that comes from love and fellowship. This lack creates a pathological anxiety to which in turn he reacts by trying to be as God. Not finding a relationship through which he can accept himself as he is and find fulfillment, he swings to a mood of ego inflation as a reaction to a deep sense of frustration of his essential being.

The Bible sees man as made in the image of God, but not as identical with God. There is a sense of living identity in terms of a vital relationship, but not an identity of being. Man is finite, limited; God is infinite, all-powerful. Man is able to love, but must first be loved and learns to love in return. God is love. The basic insight is that of a living identity but with individuality and uniqueness in both man and God; likeness, but based upon God's immeasurable greatness; similarity with profound differences. The crux of the matter is man's capacity for a relationship with God which is characterized by love and fellowship.

It is this relationship that the New Testament characterizes as Sonship. Man is a son of God, potentially through his inner capacity for identity and fellowship and actually in the measure in which he achieves this relationship. "For all who are led by the Spirit of God are sons of God." [11] The work of Christ is that of One who opens the way for turning this potential into actuality, through faith. "For in Christ Jesus you are all sons of God, through faith." [12] In one sense Sonship means a continuing life which is separate from, but like unto, the Father, unique and individual, yet with significant qualities in common, which form the basis for a living relationship releasing spiritual strength for growth and self-giving.

To illustrate through an analogy—there is a sense in which every son carries in himself the image of his father through biological inheritance. This inheritance may include certain physical features, such as color of eyes, or it may include abilities, such as musical talent. The physical features may be fixed, so that whatever the psychological relationship of son and father, the eyes remain blue. However, the full development of a musical talent, for example, will depend on the kind of relationship the boy has to his father— stimulating or repressing; encouraging or discouraging to the boy. The relation of Sonship which is made real in Christ makes possible the development of what the Old Testament calls the "image of God." Man becomes truly human only through fellowship with God as a son. God offers this possibility; man enters into it as a reality when he responds in faith, when he accepts God's acceptance of him.

But there is another side to this story of which some theologians will be quick to remind us, and which is highly important for understanding the experiences of illness and health. The Bible, being very realistic, wrestles from beginning to end with the problem of man's rebellion, destructiveness and weakness. Basically we are dealing here with the doctrine of the Fall as portrayed in the story of Adam and Eve.[13]

The basic experience for which man has to account, and with which he has to deal, is the presence within himself of forces which may be used destructively or constructively. These forces seem to be an inherent part of life. Thus all living things go through a process which eventually leads to death in the physical sense. All living things, if permitted to follow an inherent pattern of life, grow to a climax in their development and strength and then decline. Life is preserved by the reproduction of new organisms to take the place of those which are passing off the scene.

But any living organism is constantly struggling against elements in itself and in its environment which seek to destroy it. Sometimes these struggles so interfere with the functioning of the organism that the person becomes ill. When a disease such as polio attacks, the organism must marshal all of its forces to meet the attacker, and sometimes it is successful and sometimes not. And, as has been previously pointed out, it is possible for a person to use these destructive tendencies against himself, without knowing it. Much sickness grows out of a wish to be sick, and there are times when a wish to die seems to overcome the desire to live. This wish to be sick or to die may not be for sickness or death as such, but for the real or fantasied advantage accruing from such conditions.

The Bible looks upon man as destroying himself by rebelling against the law of God. Through his rebellion his relationship to God is disturbed and this brings suffering. This suffering at times has been interpreted as punishment. While not to be considered as identical, there is a close similarity between the insight of religion that the laws of God are to be obeyed and that of psychotherapy that man must accept and learn to live on the basis of reality rather than on the basis of his wishes.

It is this rebellion against the laws of God that the Bible calls sin. The concept of sin carries with it an element of responsibility on the part of the individual. Because feelings of guilt are so prominent in religious experience, and because man feels a need to be punished due to his human relationships, this element of responsibility is often distorted in the direction of punishments and blame. However, in the Christian sense man's responsibility is more that of seeking to correct the condition of sin through repentance. Likewise the physician does not blame the patient for being sick, but does expect him to take some responsibility for his cure. The individual either sinful or sick has some power of choice or decision, and this choice seems to be whether or not he will identify himself, his hopes and his goals with destructive forces or with creative elements in his experience. It is in this identification that relationships are established or broken; we feel a part of that with which we have identified and separated from that with which we have not identified. And this has a profound effect on the direction in which we are moving, either in terms of sin and salvation or of illness and health.

In dealing with destructive forces both religion and medicine have had a common general goal, that of overcoming them. Religion talks about redemption and salvation; medicine attempts to create conditions which lead to cure. In so far as the temporal life of the organism is concerned, medicine knows that it will be eventually defeated, but it seeks to prolong life. Religion sees its task in an ultimate setting of which this life is but a part. But each has taken for itself the task of helping man overcome life-destroying forces.

The central message of the Bible is concerned with this overcoming of life-destroying forces, or in other words, with salvation and redemption. It is the profound faith of the Bible in its major emphases that the creative life-giving aspects of human experience are deeper and more permanent than the destructive. Thus love is deeper than hate and may overcome hate; faith and trust save from fear. The image of God is deeper and more real than the destructive forces; indeed, the destructive aspects are at times the distortion of the image of God.

But the Bible does not portray these forces operating in life through wishful thinking or magic. We do not talk ourselves into faith or press a button which produces love. There is no easy way to overcome anxiety and no magic by which we get what we want. Infantile wishes, no matter how masked by religious approval, are in the end self-defeating. For the Bible, destructive forces are set loose by relationships that divide, isolate and separate man from man and man from God; redemptive forces find expression and release through relationships of fellowship and unity. This is the Bible's way of saying that so close is the relationship between the organism and its environment that they are one. God is one, and man experiences a redemptive relationship as he becomes one with God and with other men.

The fact that the Bible rises to its supreme height in the portrayal of the redemptive life and work of Christ is very significant for our problem. In finding the kind of relationship which releases the creative, redeeming forces in life, we need more than abstract ideas. Ideas may point a needed direction; they are not capable of reaching into the depth of the soul and bringing out redemptive responses unless they communicate a living, personal relationship. Only personality can reach the depth of other persons. In the incarnation of redemptive love in Christ, God has communicated himself on a level far deeper than words could ever penetrate. Here is One with whom each of us may identify and in that identification find release for the creative, redeeming forces within our life. Because this experience involves forces which we do not create ourselves but which operate through us, it seems as though the experience happens to us apart from our own powers. Thus we are saved by grace, by love given to us, through faith, not through our own works. But in this salvation a crucial element is the acceptance and response of faith and love to the prior love of God, and this is the place at which a profound decision takes place within us. But this decision arises from the depths outward; it cannot be forced from the outward aspects of our life toward the inner. Indeed, the Bible sees this response of faith and love as something of the work of God within us, constituting in itself something of a miracle of grace.

It is out of this profound redemptive function that the interest of the Bible in the problems of illness and health arises. Here is the source of the concern of Jesus with sick persons. For the Bible, the drama of human redemption is always lived out on the stage of the Infinite and the Eternal. When man is truly seen in this way he is also seen in the light of the drama that takes place on the level of the finite and temporal. Thus concern with sin and salvation in the larger view brings one to an interest in illness and health from the smaller perspective. Illness and health on the finite level become analogous to sin and salvation on the ultimate level. One can be interested in experiences of illness and health on purely humanitarian grounds without being interested in the ultimate problem which man faces. But one cannot be genuinely concerned with man's ultimate salvation without a living concern in the immediate problems of health. Jesus demonstrates this living concern in man's ultimate destiny expressing itself in concern for man's immediate problems.

There are several passages in St. Paul's writings which are of interest at this point. One is the passage in the Epistle to the Corinthians [14] where he says, "Do you not know that you are God's temple and that God's Spirit dwells in you? . . . For God's temple is holy, and that temple you are." What does this passage have to do with the problems of illness and health?

It is profoundly important because it deals with our basic attitude toward ourselves. What are we; only a physical being, or a physical being which has feelings and thoughts; or are we persons in whom the creative forces in this universe are trying to find expression and some measure of fulfillment? What gives man any significance he may have: what he does or what he is in relation to others and to an Ultimate Being? The Christian interpretation says the latter, and sees in Paul's figure of the temple a symbol which expresses the essential unity of man and God, a sense of God's greatness and transcendence, yet a close, living communion between God and man. Man is an expression of the creative activity of God. Man builds a temple of stone because he himself is a living temple.

This insight leads us to the idea that the life of man is a kind of language through which spiritual realities are expressed. To be able to understand the meaning of our experiences is to be able to understand how God works in human life. While some of God's ways are mysterious and beyond our reach, we certainly have at our disposal a veritable book of Life, ourselves, which if we learn to read becomes the source of profound insights.

This interpretation is confirmed in a measure by some of the insights of modern psychosomatic medicine, which views many physical symptoms as the expression of our inner spirit and attitude toward ourselves and others. This spirit grows out of our relationships with others and in turn helps to determine our relationships with others. Thus a young woman who finds her left leg paralyzed at unexpected times discovers through help that there is nothing physically wrong with the leg. The paralysis is a language through which an intense wish for love, coupled with a strong sense of guilt, is finding expression. A student finds it impossible to use his intellect on his studies and so fails in school, later to discover that he was in school only because of his mother's insistence, and that he did not really want to be there. Actually he unconsciously wanted to defeat his mother by failing. Unaware of this deeper purpose behind failure, he was nevertheless achieving it. The inhibition of intellectual powers was a language portraying his inner goals and spirit. Many things we do and many of the ways in which our bodies and minds function are really the expression of our attitudes, our values and inner spirit. To the extent that we are inwardly sick

48953

there will be some kind of an external expression of this sickness. If we can learn to read the language of the external expression of our life so that we may discern what it is saying about the internal condition, we become persons of wisdom. And this is the only way through which many troublesome symptoms of emotional and spiritual disorder can be cured.

Jesus faced this problem of the relation between external expression and internal motivation in regard to the Pharisees of his day. He tried to help them see what their beliefs and behavior were saying about their inner spirit. On one occasion he used the word "leaven" with about the same meaning as the word "spirit" is used here. "Beware of the leaven of the Pharisees, which is hypocrisy. Nothing is covered up that will not be revealed, or hidden that will not be known. Whatever you have said in the dark shall be heard in the light, and what you have whispered in private rooms shall be proclaimed upon the housetops." [15] It would be easy to read into the thinking of Jesus the modern idea of unconscious mental processes which express themselves in external behavior. This is one of the basic ideas on which the approach of modern science to the problems of emotional illness is grounded. And certainly we know that one of our very common emotional and spiritual ailments grows out of our need to cover up painful and undesirable elements in the deeper levels of our life by putting on behavior which is exactly the opposite in character. We rely heavily on the acceptance of, and conformity to, external forms and creeds to assure ourselves that we do not have to look more deeply into ourselves. Jesus also stated this central idea when he said, "The good man out of the good treasure of his heart produces good, and the evil man out of his evil treasure produces evil; for out of the abundance of the heart his mouth speaks." [16] There is no substitute for being genuine, and the behavior of a man expresses what he genuinely is.

There is also a positive side of this relationship between external expression and inner condition. The deepest, most creative energies of our bodies and minds find their fullest life as expressions of such spiritual qualities as love, faith, hope, courage. It is common knowledge that an all-consuming purpose which rises from the depth of one's being can release and unite energies and abilities for what may seem to others superhuman efforts and achievements. Studies of the aging process in human beings indicate, for example, that the crucial problem is what might be called the aging of the spirit. Where the inner meaning and direction of a life is strong, and where there are meaningful goals to be achieved, physical health and well-being may be greatly facilitated.

It should be evident that we are not thinking of spirit as a sort of disembodied, ethereal ghost which inhabits the thin air and which may somehow get inside of us. We are thinking of spirit as the expression of our central attitudes and values; it is a word or symbol through which we express our understanding of the character of a person as this is revealed in his goals and in the manner in which he pursues his goals. In the Bible, as in life, there is always the suggestion of power in the meaning of this word, and it is power in which certain ends or goals are inherent.

The Bible recognizes good and evil spirits. Indeed, many sick persons were said to be possessed by an evil or unclean spirit, or by a demon. Jesus is said to have cast out evil spirits, and the disciples were given power to cast out unclean spirits and to heal diseases. It is evident from reading these sections of the Gospels that Jesus was here dealing with persons suffering from what today we would call neuroses and psychoses, persons who were "out of their mind," as we say; persons in whom destructive energies have overcome creative energies, whose life and energies are not organized and directed toward satisfying goals. The approach which Jesus made to these persons was one of deep understanding and love, and it is evident from our psychological knowledge today that any who would help the mentally ill must be persons of deep understanding and love.

But Paul speaks of the Spirit of God dwelling in us. The Spirit of God is a major theme in the Bible, the adequate and comprehensive development of which would require extensive discussion. However, we need to bear in mind that one way the Bible seeks to portray the close relationship which may exist between God and man is through this idea of spirit. This relationship is more than closeness; it is one through which the good potentialities of man's life become actual.

The believer is to be "strengthened with might through his Spirit in the inner man." [17] "The fruit of the Spirit is love, joy, peace, patience, kindness, goodness, faithfulness, gentleness, self-control." [18] Thus the Bible sees the life of righteousness in man as something which is not man-made, but rather the product of the Spirit of God working within man, requiring the response of the spirit of man.

This Biblical idea is not unlike the modern psychological idea that we grow as persons in and through our relationship with other persons; that as these relationships lead to a sense of security and adequacy we grow in the direction of health; as these relationships lead to a sense of anxiety, guilt or hostility we tend to become ill. What we are or what we become is in part determined by what we take into ourselves of the feelings and attitudes of others toward us. The spirit of others, if evil, tends to create evil feelings in us, especially in childhood; if good, that is, loving and accepting, it tends to create a good spirit within us. No man is only himself; he is himself in and through a dynamic relationship with others by means of which he is being strengthened in what he is, or by means of which he is being changed. Perhaps the figure of leaven which Jesus used expresses this thought in part, except that the spirit of man is not to be thought of as something which passively accepts the influence of another, but rather actively responds to it, and in responding is changed.

We may get a sense of the vitality of the experience of the early Jewish Christians by remembering that they had come up through a system of rigid legalism which had offered them salvation through a strict obedience to codes of external behavior. The experience which was theirs through their faith in Christ was that of being released from this legalism to a life committed to Christ in love. This release led to a kind of spontaneity and vitality which is evident on the pages of the New Testament. Their new life was something which they did not give to themselves; it came through Christ. Being a deep, inward experience they could talk of it only through words which expressed this inwardness, and the Spirit of God dwelling in them became a form for the expression of this experience. That this experience led them to make a full response of their whole being in an increasingly active manner is evident from their lives. It led them into difficulty and trouble and hardship and struggle; not to an easy peace of mind. Jesus himself "was led up by the Spirit into the wilderness to be tempted by the devil." [19] This temptation was the facing of very profound issues which involved his destiny as the Son of God. Anyone who finds himself growing because of experiences of love given to him by others also finds it necessary to face those forces within himself which lead him to respond to love in an unloving manner. In the New Testament this was temptation; in modern parlance we call it inner conflict.

This brings us to one of the differences between Biblical thought and modern psychology which needs to be understood. The Bible is not interested primarily in interpreting man, as is modern psychology. The Bible is interested primarily in interpreting the life of God in the life of man. Modern psychology is interested in interpreting man as man, and seeks to make the interpretation without reference to God. It therefore seems to be humanistic, and sometimes is so. In their own way both Biblical thought and modern science are being true to their essential nature and purpose. Modern Christians misuse psychological thought when they seek to use it to prove their faith. Faith must rest on other grounds. Psychology, on the other hand, misuses its function when it seeks to disprove faith. Psychology can tell us a great deal about the way in which we comprehend and respond to anything with which we have a living relationship, such as a child to a mother. Psychologists see a great many persons who comprehend and respond to God in a very childish, dependent manner, expecting God to solve all of their problems for them and deliver them from all evil and suffering and give them a life of ease which is the absence of struggle. Psychology points out the need of being able to use the powers of intelligence, creativity and love to the full, and also the kind of human relationships which must exist if this is to be achieved. What psychologists describe is very much like the experience to which the New Testament witnesses as the Spirit of God in man. In each case the individual is related to something or someone outside himself—either human or divine—but the nature of the relationship is such that it both requires and makes possible the full response of the person and the full use of his powers and abilities in a relationship of giving as well as of receiving. This is responsibility within a framework of mutual interdependency; not passivity within a framework of child-ish dependency.

At this point a question presents itself: How did the writers of the New Testament know so much about the Spirit of God? Only in and through their experience. Being religious men they accepted themselves as creatures of God and saw everything which took place within their experience as speaking something about the way God works in human life. They saw their life in the perspective of an eternal and cosmic purpose of which they were a small part, a pur-pose which was working out through them, as their life was being worked out through it. Their concept of cause was different from that of the modern scientist, who sees cause and effect relationships on the level of everyday experiences and relationships. The Bible also portrays this immediate level of cause and effect; "whatever a man sows, that he will also reap." [20] And the Bible as well as psychology points out that whatever is sown in a man, that shall he also reap, unless he does something to change the effect of this sowing. Here is the meaning of the idea of repentance; that we take responsibility for the evil in ourselves even though it may grow in part out of our reaction to the attitudes of others toward us. This reaction can be changed, but only in and through loving, healing, saving relationships with others. Paul points out that we may sow to the flesh, a word that is often misinterperted to mean the body. Instead, it refers to certain characteristics of the whole person which are destructive, or to our ability to respond to our experiences in ways that are destructive of ourselves and others. Actually, Paul's description of the works of the flesh closely resembles modern descriptions of symptoms of neuroses and other forms of emotional illness, such as alcoholism. Or we may sow to the Spirit, and here the fruits are described in terms much like some psychiatrists use in describing a mature person. Up to a point the individual has a choice, whether he is choosing between illness or health, or sin or salvation. The Bible presents experiences on the human level as expressing and portraying truth about God and the ways in which God works in human life. The Biblical faith would not fear the so-called humanism of modern psychology because it would say that whatever of truth psychology discovers about man reflects God's activity in the life of man and man's response to this activity, whether the psychologist sees it in these terms or not. And it would also point out that there is nothing in human relationships which is not significant for man's relationships with God the Supreme Person. Human experience is always an analogy through which faith sees beyond the finite to the infinite. "Do you not know that you are God's temple and that God's Spirit dwells in you?"

There are other implications of this interpretation. One is in regard to our attitudes toward our bodies and their functioning. If the body is the temple of God then there is nothing in the body which is in itself evil or which should cause guilt by its possession. For instance, sex. Sex is part of God's creation and it is part of the life of God in man and should be used as such. To be sure, it can be used for destructive ends, and this occurs when its expression is governed by such motives as fear or exploitation rather than by mature love. Psychotherapists think of persons who use sex destructively as sick persons; religion is likely to think of them as sinful; in either case the answer involves a fundamental change—a change in the central motives and goals rather than merely a change in behavior. The Christian faith has a definite contribution to the prevention and cure of much illness by helping us to grow into the experience of accepting ourselves and all aspects of ourselves in the light of our fullest potentialities. Paul expresses this idea in terms of being the temple, the dwelling-place of the Spirit of God, and hence holy.

The word "holy" has more than one connotation. In some connections it means the transcendent, the "wholly other." But there is also another meaning which is important in this particular context. In this meaning the word "holy" may be related to two other words, "health" and "wholeness." To be healthy is to be a living whole. To be healthy is to experience all of our parts functioning in such a way that each of them makes their particular contribution to the welfare of the whole. The various organs of the body cannot function properly unless they are united and integrated by the brain and nervous system. But integration requires more than the mere physical functioning of the brain, because this functioning is influenced by feelings which are the experience of the whole person. So wholeness is in part a matter of feelings; anxiety tears apart, trust makes whole. So wholeness is also a matter of the kind of relationships we receive from others and give to others; these may tear apart or separate us from others, or they may bind together as in a fellowship. The Bible understands a quality of relationship which is "holy" because it makes for reconciliation and belonging. It sees this as grounded in the attitude of God toward men which becomes a motivation and pattern for the relation of the Christian to his fellow men. This is spiritual wholeness, or holiness. On our part it is at least an attitude of open trust and self-giving love toward God that finds expression toward others. It is possible to seek a kind of false holiness through a relationship with God which insulates us from our fellows. It is also possible to seek wholeness through human relationships alone. But holiness in the Biblical sense involves both of these dimensions.

In the Christian message reconciliation and belonging are offered for our acceptance or rejection. Our response is the crucial factor. We can accept only as we have insight into our need. This is apparently what Jesus had in mind when he said, "The eye is the lamp of the body. So, if your eye is sound, your whole body will be full of light; but if your eye is not sound, your whole body will be full of darkness. If then the light in you is darkness, how great is the darkness!" [21] Here is clearly stated the possibility of man's gaining insight into his need or keeping himself blinded to his need. To gain insight means to see and to be willing to give up or modify those aspects of our inner life which keep us from wholeness in all of our relationships. This task is at times difficult and painful. It is the difference between maintaining a condition of sin, in the sense of separation and inner disunity, or moving toward salvation in the sense of a redemptive relationship with our fellow men and with

God. Insight which leads to the acceptance of the love which is offered us is the road to spiritual health or holiness. The emotionally and spiritually unhealthy person may have difficulty in seeing his need and because of this difficulty may become more unhealthy. Holiness is a continual movement toward spiritual health grounded in insight into our constant needs and our willingness to accept the love of God which provides the belonging we need in order to become our true selves.

The insights of the Bible are expressed in vivid symbols such as the "temple of God," or the "eye" or "light" and "darkness," and many others. Therefore some understanding of the nature of religious symbols is helpful in their interpretation. Any creative religious writer seeks to formulate deep, intangible but profoundly significant meanings which he has experienced. These intangible meanings cannot be expressed directly or literally, but only through symbols. The deeper meanings of religious experience must be expressed in symbols which are taken from the external world but used in a way that seeks to express inner relationships and meanings. For instance, Paul speaks about man as a temple. Now if this is taken literally it makes no sense. Rather it is to be used as an analogy, as an image through which a deeper truth is communicated on the level of feelings as well as of ideas. To try to make a literal interpretation of what Paul meant is to miss the point completely, as a literal interpretation of the meaning of a great work of art would miss its deeper meaning. Religious symbols are like windows through which we may look into our own souls and into the nature and meaning of life. It is not the symbol which is important, but what the author is trying to say through the symbol. Our task is to approach the symbol with receptivity, imagination and feeling as well as reason, and in this way come to "see" its meaning rather than to arrive at "logical conclusions."

In another passage Paul uses the symbol of gifts. In I Corinthians 12:4–31, he develops the idea that the many abilities of man are gifts, that their common source is the activity of God, that there is something of a mystery about it all. The word he uses to denote that common source is "Spirit." This speaks of God's relationship to man. We feel these gifts within ourselves, we know they are there, and under certain conditions may be used, but we know also that they are not of our own making. The common root is the creative power of God, and Spirit is God working in and through human life for the common good. It is this sense of our own rootage in a Power infinitely beyond ourselves that prevents a false pride and gives our life an ultimate significance. But we must also use these gifts for the common good in daily relationships, else we do not find fulfillment and become ill.

Paul continues his thought by interpreting the church through symbols which grow out of insight into the nature of our physical existence; for instance, his understanding of the nature of the body as a totality having many parts, each part making its contribution to the whole, no part more or less significant than another, and each part so related to the others that when one suffers, all suffer. Paul is calling attention to the fact that there is an inherent wholeness in life and to the extent that this wholeness is destroyed the person or group is ill. This basic idea of modern psychosomatic medicine was also known and discussed among the Greeks, and it is possible that Paul, educated as he was, had some knowledge of Greek thinking at this point. On the other hand, the Old Testament also assumes a unity or wholeness within man, and certainly Paul was familiar with this fact. From whatever source, it is an insight which is receiving great emphasis today. When we achieve oneness within ourselves, with our fellow men, and with God we have achieved our highest state of health and well-being. This is really to be holy—but it may be far from being pious or from being a conformist. For to be whole means both to be related in love with our fellow men and with God, and through this relationship find full expression of our individuality.

## Chapter Two

# Fear, Anxiety and Faith

JOHN consulted his pastor, saying that he was very fearful. He found himself worried about his job and his work, about finances, about the children, about some things in himself, but mostly about his wife. At times he felt that something serious might happen to her, and if it did, he could not endure the experience. He asked his pastor what he could do to overcome all these fears.

John was truly afraid, but he was not suffering from what is usually called real fear. This does not mean that his experience was imaginary. He was very much upset, but he was suffering from what is called anxiety. Until a clear distinction is made between these two types of feeling, we cannot understand our fears and anxieties, nor can we understand the relation of religion to them.

Fear is a word usually used to describe a response to a real threat to our life or person. The feeling which we have standing in the middle of the road watching an automobile approach at high speed could be labeled fear. The automobile is a real danger to life and limb. Mrs. Overstreet, in her excellent book, *Understanding Fear in Ourselves and Others*,[1] cites some real dangers of which we in our society need to be afraid, among them tendencies in our own minds which make us blind at points where we should see, and tendencies to follow irrational rather than intelligent forms of self-defense. We need also to be afraid of the authoritarian personality who wants to take control over the lives of other people, and of those groups which want to take over our free institutions. We need also to fear a sense of helplessness that says there is little we can do as citizens to correct many of our common problems. These things are threats to our individual, social, political, and religious life.

There is a protective aspect in real fear that is valuable both to the individual and to society. Fear stimulates the adrenal glands and prepares the organism for action. Real dangers can be dealt with either by fight or by flight. One would hardly think of fighting the speeding automobile, but with some other real dangers, flight would not be the intelligent, appropriate, constructive answer. Fear serves a valuable purpose in helping us to meet real dangers, when it is combined with intelligent understanding of the situation. Fear is the awareness of a real danger created by a specific object or situation where the feeling is in proportion to the actual danger.

Sometimes there are problems in distinguishing between fears and anxiety. Often a person is observed on a street corner, looking right, then left, at the approaching cars, obviously afraid to start across the street. After making several false starts, he suddenly dashes across at a moment when a car is very near to him. It could be said that his fears are so strong that they interfere with the proper use of his intelligence. While he would say that he is afraid of being hit, one might also suspect that there are other elements in his feelings more in the nature of anxieties.

Again, children are often made afraid of the wrong thing. A mother, seeing her little child too close to the hot stove, may slap the child's hand. In her fear she seeks to make the child afraid of the stove, but she actually makes him afraid of her. Now a hot stove is a danger to a child, but a less fearful approach on the part of the mother would help the child to understand that it is the stove and not the mother of which he should beware. Her approach disturbs his sense of security and his relationship with her, and hence develops anxiety.

The meaning of anxiety is different from fear. In our previous illustration, John was anxious. The things that he worried about were not the real basis for his feelings. What had happened to John?

There had been a period in his life when he had felt very resentful toward his wife. She did things which he did not like. At the time he was aware of this resentment. The more he brooded about her activities, the more resentful he became. Later he remembered having had some fears about his resentment. He wondered then whether these feelings could ever get out of hand so that he actually might hurt her. He sensed a danger in the way he felt. But as time went on he found himself becoming less resentful, consciously. Still, while he did not feel so resentful toward her, he noticed himself becoming more worried about her. Plainly his resentment was pushed to the rear of his mind, and in its place he became aware of this growing sense of anxiety. Previously, he had felt guilty about his resentment; now he felt that his concern was the expression of affection for his wife.

John's experience is a good illustration of the basic meaning of anxiety. Although somewhat oversimplified, the basic facts remain true. Anxiety is a panic reaction to something that does not constitute an actual danger to our life, but does constitute a danger to our inner being, to our self. In John's case anxiety was a symptom of the deeper problem of resentment. Thus we see that for John one part of himself was threatened by another part of himself. Not being aware of the real cause of his anxiety, he was unable to do anything constructive about it.

Anxiety, then, is a state of tension created by conditions which constitute a threat to the self. Here the word "self" refers not only to the body, but rather to what religious people have referred to as the soul. It is our essential being, our basic attitudes toward ourselves, others, life in general, God, as these attitudes are organized into a functioning whole out of which our behavior is motivated. Perhaps the very core of the self is the sense of security which we feel in and through our various relationships with others. The awareness of our meaning, value or worth to others is an important aspect of the self, since out of this awareness come our feelings of security.

A speeding automobile may threaten physical harm or even bodily death, and because death is a threat to the existence of the self, it may create anxiety. However, most of our anxiety grows out of situations which do not threaten physical existence or even bodily harm, but rather threaten to destroy the meanings around which our lives are organized, the values or satisfactions which we seek in our relationships with others, our sense of personal worth, our basic security. Security is always security-with-another.

Anxiety then is a sense of inner danger. A man may have knowledge of a business situation which makes him realize that he has a good chance of losing his capital. Under the stimulus of this fear he may set about to salvage what he can, to plan ways of recouping his loss, and he may learn from the experience. Or he may become panicky. He may feel that life has lost all of its meaning, that he is a complete failure, and that there is no use to go on living. Here the loss of his money is more than just the loss of money; it is a blow to his self, to the values in which he found security and strength. Having lost his source of security, there is nothing to live for. He experiences anxiety.

Fear is a very specific feeling related to a specific threatening object or situation. Anxiety is a generalized sense of panic. It may be related to persons or situations, but it is also related to feelings, values and attitudes which the person finds within himself. Thus much of our anxiety today is due to strong feelings of resentment which threaten to get out of control. This brings on a sort of "all gone feeling," a sense of helplessness and impotence, of futility and confusion.

One source of anxiety is our relationship with other persons. We have various kinds of relationships with the people with whom we have to live. When anything in these relationships becomes a threat to our physical or emotional well-being, then we have a basis for anxiety. When our relationships with others are characterized by understanding, affection and security, they give no basis for anxiety.

Children, for example, need to feel deeply loved, accepted and wanted. When they do not feel this love they are in a state of tension which we call anxiety. This anxiety may express itself in various kinds of behavior. A child who withdraws from others and wants to play by himself is usually an anxious child. On the other hand, aggressive, destructive behavior in children may also be rooted in anxiety growing out of faulty parental relationships. Some children become submissive and passive in relationships which produce anxiety, while others rebel, become hostile and overly aggressive.

Early infancy is an especially critical time from the point of view of developing either anxiety or trust in a child. The infant before birth has been in a state of warmth and close physical union with the mother. At birth he becomes a different organism, separate but still dependent on others, particularly on the mother. The primary way in which this dependency is felt is through his need for food and love. Love must be given with his food. He also needs warmth, a feeling that he is in tender hands, a feeling of safety. If he feels unloved, or lack of genuine warmth, or a sense of coldness or hostility, he will become tense. This tension is an expression of anxiety. To the extent that he is anxious, he will not be able to trust those about him.

The relation of some childhood fears and anxieties to adult anxieties now begins to come clear. A child may have a real fear of his father, because of the father's hostile, punishing attitude. He may then struggle within himself, not wanting to be afraid, or he may be aware of hostile feelings toward his father and may sense that if he expresses this hostility he will be punished. Thus he is afraid of something outside himself, but also of something inside himself. He has both fear and anxiety. Next he may develop a fear of the dark, or a fear of animals, or of some other object which has no real danger for him; such feelings are actually anxieties because the objects do not constitute the real source of his feelings. He has shifted his feelings from his father to these other objects. When a real fear is so separated from the external cause of the feelings and is experienced as related to a symbolic cause, such as the dark, the term anxiety is more appropriate. Many of the anxieties that plague adults are carried up from childhood and are expressed in adult life in a disguised and distorted form.

In such anxiety there is obviously an unhealthy condition. The child is unable to relate his feelings to the real cause, and therefore he is incapacitated for handling his feelings constructively. Parents who try to reassure such children that there is nothing of which to be afraid, and who urge them to be brave, are surprised that their reassurances are ineffective. This is because the child is experiencing strong tension, and as long as he is experiencing it, it is futile to tell him that there is no reason for it. In fact, such procedures usually increase his anxiety, for they indicate that the parent does not understand. In adult life such verbal reassurance is likewise futile.

Adults are anxious about many things. A man, for example, was afraid of his employer. Sometimes in his fear he reacted rather violently against the employer. He feared the employer would be unjust, would criticize him, would not promote him. On the other hand, he said he had no real reason to feel this way; after all, the employer was a pretty decent fellow. It took some help to discover that the root of his problem was fear of his father. In childhood he had had reason to be afraid of his father; so now he was afraid of one who stood in a similar position of authority. When he saw the connection, and not until he saw it and worked through it, the anxiety of adult life disappeared, and he was able to trust the employer.

Many adult anxieties are formed on this basis. Experiences and relationships which aroused fear or anxiety in childhood become buried in the deeper parts of the mind, and the person "forgets" them; that is, he is no longer aware of them. But the memory is still there in terms of a more or less clear feeling of apprehension, which becomes attached to some adult relationship that is similar to the childhood relationship.

During the past decade or two parents have been made very much aware of the direct results of their attitudes toward the child. Society always needs someone to blame, and parents are pretty good scapegoats, especially since so much guilt can be proved. But there is one catch. Parents tend to rear their children as they are taught to rear them. And they are taught in the early years of their own childhood, not intellectually, but emotionally, in relationship with their own parents. They usually learn well, too well, and often learn harmful attitudes. But they do not realize that their attitudes are harmful or why they are harmful. Furthermore, they have not been helped to change their attitudes. This is the place where society faces a responsibility.

But the attitude that "the parent is to blame" only creates anxiety in parents and puts them on the defensive, thus making the situation worse. When society realizes that in condemning parents it is really condemning itself and in helping parents it is really helping itself, some constructive changes will be made. Many parents want help. Being human they can work out their problems and change their attitudes only in a community relationship of acceptance and understanding, not in a community of blame. Sometimes expert help is needed, just as it is for children. Acceptance, not blame, is basic to the solution of anxiety at any age level.

As we have seen, one source of anxiety lies in our relationships with other persons. Another source is in our relationships with ourselves. In other words, sometimes we are anxious because one part of our inner self is threatening another part. The conflict is within us; and anxiety is a symptom of the conflict. In the case of John, already mentioned, a large part of his anxiety was a reaction to his feelings of hostility.

Some people are very anxious about their sexual feelings. Their conscience and their sexual feelings are in conflict; they feel strong guilt in relation to sex. The feeling of guilt may go back to childhood teachings, or to relationships with parents in which they were made to feel guilt about sex, or to some other kind of sexual experience. Or the basis of the guilt feeling may be in their attitudes toward their parents. A man, for example, who is too closely attached to his mother emotionally may feel anxious about sexual relationships with his wife.

Under certain circumstances anger, resentment and sex become one factor in the creation of anxiety; the other factor being something from the environment or from another aspect of the personality, such as conscience, with which these feelings of anger or sex are in conflict and by which they are condemned. Our society and our churches have attempted to help persons control these impulses by teaching that they are evil, and fail to give more constructive help. We are learning today that this kind of teaching both fails to control them and does severe damage to personality. We need to learn a better method for handling these impulses.

There is another side of the picture, too. People may develop anxieties about the positive side of their life. They want to love, for example, in the tender, self-giving sense. They realize somewhat the values of such love both for themselves and others. But they are inhibited by anxieties developed in some earlier experience, when they have tried to be tender to someone only to get pushed away or hurt. Also, in order to control the behavior of children, parents often make them afraid to express some ability or talent; then in later life the individual so repressed may feel anxious because he cannot do something which he very much wants and needs to do. Many anxious people say, "I wish I could do this, but every time I try I get so disturbed." Many people want to be Christian in the deep and genuine sense of showing real love toward others, but when they attempt to do so they become anxious and therefore inhibited.

Thus far we have been thinking about anxiety which is the result of our relationships with others, induced by situations which we almost literally take within our personalities where they continue to affect us long after the actual relationship which produced them has been forgotten. There is also another kind of anxiety, which grows out of the basic conditions of life or is inherent in the very nature of life.

A theologian, Dr. Paul Tillich,[2] has carefully worked out the nature of this kind of anxiety, distinguishing three types, but indicating that they are very closely related.

The first is the anxiety of fate and death. To be alive is to face the possibility of death, of nonexistence. To be alive is to feel dependent on many elements beyond our control. A common form of expressing this anxiety is by the question, Is the universe friendly or unfriendly to human life? or, If a man die, shall he live again?

The second basic kind of anxiety is that of emptiness and meaninglessness. At the very center of his life man must find a meaning which organizes and gives purpose and value to his multitudinous activities, else all is empty and void. Lack of such meaning gives a sense of isolation, and isolation always means anxiety. But one does not create such a center by force of will or intention; it is rather as one is able to give himself in love and trust to the God who is the ultimate source of his being, that he finds this kind of significance.

The third kind of basic anxiety is that of guilt and condemnation, not so much condemnation from one's fellows, as a facing of the question. What have I done with that which was given me? This anxiety grows out of our knowledge that life is a gift, and that we have a responsibility in the fulfillment of our potentialities.

There is no doubt but that these basic anxieties become entangled with anxieties which grow out of our relationships with others. As a matter of fact, parents may pass these anxieties on to their children quite as readily as they may pass on an anxiety about sex, or anxiety about sex may partake of these basic anxieties and lead to the feeling that life itself is dependent on having certain sexual satisfactions. But it is unlikely that these basic anxieties will become neurotic, that is, lead to an illness, unless there are also other deep anxieties growing out of our interpersonal relationships.

Practically all persons have anxiety, and easy prescriptions for ridding oneself of anxiety just do not comprehend the facts. Perhaps there is an analogy in physical illness. A specific illness may be cured; but the conditions for illness are always present and we must be constantly overcoming these conditions. So, too, our life is spent in constant necessity to overcome conditions which create some kind of anxiety.

How can we tell one kind of anxiety from another? This is indeed a difficult task. Where anxiety has become a problem we can be sure that much of it has grown out of relationships between persons, and this is an immediate and fruitful place to begin investigation. Sometimes when a person gains relief from a specific anxiety, he finds strength to handle other anxieties. Sometimes it is a problem to discover just what it is that one is anxious about, for we have a way of shifting our feelings from their real to more easily acceptable origins. Persons who have an active trust which relates them in a growing manner to everyday reality and to God have here a source of strength for facing anxieties. Such trust helps them to discover what anxieties can be eliminated through the correction of faulty relationships and values, and what anxieties are to be overcome by a living faith. But this kind of trust is not to be confused with what is currently called "thinking positively" or with other such easy reassurances.

From this discussion it may seem as though anxiety is both normal and abnormal, and so it is. It is like the temperature of the body; we must have some, but if it gets too high we are sick. Everyone has experiences which create some anxiety; some have experiences which create very intense anxiety, and this may cause sickness. Anxiety is very appropriate in some situations, such as in a soldier in a battle line, but it is not appropriate in a man walking down a main street in daylight. Anxiety which is inappropriate is abnormal. Some persons may have intense anxiety, but also strength enough to control it. Nevertheless, they should take appropriate steps to reduce its intensity, rather than seek to justify its existence. Others cannot keep the anxiety from controlling them. This is sickness. The healthy person is aware of the origins of his anxiety, and hence sees the directions in which answers lie. When the person is not aware of the origins of his anxiety he tends to become sick by confusing substitutes for the real origins.

Some observers say that anxiety is our most pressing problem today. In the light of these insights into the nature of anxiety we turn to the insights of the Bible.

*Fear, Anxiety and the Bible*

The oldest book in our Bible was written in the eighth century B.C.; the most recent was written about one hundred fifty years A.D. The material in the Bible, therefore, covers a span of roughly one thousand years and records the life of a people living in a culture far different from our own. Yet the Bible presents the problem of anxiety just as vividly and intensely as we know it today. When we get the feeling that no people ever knew anxiety as we know it today, we may turn to the Bible for a correction of our perspective.

The Bible speaks freely of fear and anxiety. "The fear of the Lord is the beginning of wisdom." "Do not be anxious about your life." "And do not fear those who kill the body but cannot kill the soul; rather fear him who can destroy both soul and body in hell. Are not two sparrows sold for a penny? And not one of them will fall to the ground without your Father's will. But even the hairs of your head are all numbered. Fear not, therefore; you are of more value than many sparrows." "Martha, Martha, you are anxious and troubled about many things." "Have no anxiety about anything. . . ." "There is no fear in love, but perfect love casts out fear. For fear has to do with punishment, and he who fears is not perfected in love." [3]

The Bible speaks also of faith. Indeed, the Bible can be called a book of faith. One of its dominant themes is the trustworthiness of God. "The Lord is my shepherd, I shall not want." "Your faith has made you well; go in peace, and be healed of your disease." "Faith is the assurance of things hoped for, the conviction of things not seen." [4]

Many people in a state of fear and anxiety read the Bible to find help or relief. Some find that the passages they read intensify their anxieties. With some there seems to be no effect. With others, there is a strong feeling of relief. When we are fearful or anxious it is sometimes easy to find material which seems to make us more anxious. On the other hand, when some persons are anxious their mind does not seem to absorb ideas.

Those who find help in Scripture passages seem to be of two kinds. One has anxieties but is also capable of some basic trust. Reading the Bible seems to strengthen the trusting elements of his personality, so that he is able to face his fears and anxieties, and although he may go through a severe struggle, he does succeed in some measure in mastering some of the situations which cause painful feelings.

Another kind of person who seems to find help is fearful or anxious, but he feels that he should not be that way, and he is looking for help in pushing these unacceptable feelings out of his mind. Biblical passages seem to tell him that he should not fear or be anxious, that these feelings are wrong, that he should have faith. Sometimes he learns to say certain passages that suggest faith over and over to himself. When he has these passages in his attention, and perhaps for a period afterward, he does not feel anxiety. But he has to repeat this process, and he may find his anxieties returning at times in such force that they completely push all thoughts of faith and trust in God out of his mind. Then he may indeed feel helpless. This process of repressive self-suggestion, though widely advised and practiced, is unhealthy because it does not lead us to face and resolve those anxieties which can be resolved or to live with those which cannot. It may be like taking an aspirin for a headache and ignoring a deep-seated infection that is causing the headache.

There is a very good reason why we turn to the Bible for help. To understand this reason will help us understand how we should use the Bible for real help, for the reason lies in part in the nature and character of the Bible itself.

The Bible is an account of the spiritual struggle of individuals and groups over a number of centuries. It portrays in vivid form experiences of fear and anxiety, hostility and guilt, faith and trust, love and forgiveness, and other profound attitudes and feelings. Here we find man at his lowest and at his highest, at his worst and at his best, portrayed concretely in language that communicates below the level of abstract ideas. The language of the Bible is heavily weighted with profound insights into the nature of life.

It is because the experiences portrayed in the Bible are similar to our own experiences that we can identify ourselves with its characters. Profound expressions of faith strike a responsive chord within us. The Bible portrays our problems and speaks of creative answers in terms which we can understand. It tells us most eloquently that God, on whom we are dependent for life, can be trusted.

What does it mean to say that the Bible is the Word of God? It means at least this—that the Bible reveals the processes and relationships in life which destroy personality, and also the processes and relationships which create personality and make possible its most complete development. "The Word of God" symbolically expresses the profound relationships between man and God, man and his fellow men, man and himself, and emphasizes that these realities are of God's creation and that God reveals himself through them. Because of its nature, the Bible does not reward the hasty glance with deep and abiding insight. Neither does it prevent the person who does not want insight and understanding from using its passages to cover up and avoid his real problem. The Bible is true to life in that like life, it can be used in any manner that one desires to use it, or is able to use it. The key is the person who uses the Bible.

The reader and what he brings to his reading is important for any book, but very important for the Bible, for here the reader must give himself to its message in a receptive, imaginative, sensitive manner. He must want to see what it is driving at and be open to new insights into himself even though they are painful, and above all he has to be ready to revise or change his attitudes and actions in the direction of those insights. The possibility of a creative identification with Christ, through which we grow toward the ideal which he revealed, gives the Bible a value above all other books. But the reader must participate openly in making this possibility effective.

## The Bible and Anxiety

One of the first expressions of the problem of anxiety which we meet in the Bible is the story of Adam and Eve.[5] Their basic anxiety needs to be distinguished from their fear of punishment, which fear is very common in persons who are conscious that they have wronged someone.

The basic anxiety is expressed in the first part of the story where we see Eve arguing with the serpent. The first problem here is the anxiety which Eve feels because of her finiteness; she cannot accept the limitation of being human. Man is not all-powerful, and sometimes it bothers him that he is not. Only God is all-powerful; man is finite, weak, limited, and he wants to become as God. Here is one kind of anxiety which grows out of our fundamental nature. We face certain insecurities because there are aspects of life which we cannot control, and which have the power to destroy us. This is what was called "basic" anxiety in the previous section.

The kind of anxiety which grows out of inner conflict that is a threat to the self is also implicit in this powerful portrayal of human experience. By means of conversation with a second party, the serpent, Eve deals with her anxiety. If we are to understand this story psychologically, we should see the serpent as a symbol of one part of Eve which is having a sort of tug-of-war with another part, identified as desire and conscience. The author of the story has made a very clever literary use of a psychological process—the process by which we project on to something in the external world, even to the extent of personifying an object such as a serpent, some aspect of our inner feelings or impulses which we cannot accept as a part of ourselves.

The point of this conversation is that Eve succeeded in persuading herself that the demands of reality—the command of God that the fruit of this tree should not be eaten—were not applicable to her, and so developed in fantasy the belief that she could disregard the command of God with impunity. The conversation is a beautiful illustration of the process by which we rationalize our anxieties. Part of this process consists in building up a false sense of immunity to the natural consequences of our behavior.

To put the conflict more specifically: Eve was troubled, anxious because something was forbidden. She was troubled, not only because of her apparent powerlessness, but because the probibition interfered with her desire. Had she had no desire there would have been no temptation, no anxiety, no conversation to record. The serpent—one part of her—begins by calling the situation into question. Conscience replies by reiterating the command of God. Anxiety arises because of the threat of condemnation and punishment. But the part of her which desires the forbidden fruit succeeds in persuading the part of her which wants to accept the reality of God's command that not punishment, but benefits, will come from the forbidden act. In gaining knowledge of good and evil she would be able to overcome finite limitations and become like God in at least one important aspect of life. It is this tendency of anxiety to lead man in his weakness to unreal and fantastic solution of conflict situations that results in what the theologians have called sin and what the physicians have called illness. We do not mean here to equate "sin" and "illness," but only to indicate a common basic root, anxiety.

Anxiety is always a large element in temptation, for temptation always involves choice. There are the possibilities of a right and a wrong decision, a beneficial and a harmful action, and a sense that one is free to go either way. The conflict and the anxiety resulting from it and from the necessity of exercising one's freedom may so confuse the person that he is driven to an impulsive action which turns out to be the wrong decision. Only in wholeness is there strength. The anxiety which is felt after the act is the recognition that what we feel to be reality has been violated and that real danger may result from our choice.

Another aspect of anxiety is illustrated in this story. Anxiety is often considered as the primary evil; it is said that anxiety makes us sick. There is a certain truth in this statement but a deeper truth lies behind it, for the problem of anxiety is basically one of relationships—in this story the relationship of Eve to God and to certain aspects of her own personality. The relationship was not whole, there was a lack of unity. This distinction between anxiety being the major evil, and anxiety being a symptom of a faulty relationship is important in considering how to deal with anxiety. Many times, both in religious experience and otherwise, we attempt to deal with anxiety as though it were the thing of major importance, and as though all we need to do is to calm our anxieties, but anxieties are never really calmed until the relationships out of which they arise are changed or understood.

In the story of Esau's [6] selling his birthright we have another illustration of the insight of ancient religious writers into the nature of anxiety. A somewhat different aspect is emphasized, but the difference is mainly in emphasis. Again we see desire, the normal desire for food that a hungry man knows, in conflict with a potential value which the man possesses, his birthright. The fact that scholars are not too clear on the exact historical or cultural significance of the birthright need not keep us from seeing the psychological significance. Every human being has a birthright—that of a mature personality—simply by virtue of the fact that he has been born. But every human being does not achieve this birthright. One reason for this failure is clearly seen in the Esau story.

Becoming mature involves developing the latent capacity for postponing immediate gratification of desires in order to achieve a larger or fuller satisfaction later. Or it involves developing the capacity to endure tension or hunger and its resultant suffering now in order to avoid a greater suffering later. This capacity to postpone satisfaction or endure suffering comes in conflict with an immature impulse in personality which demands the immediate satisfaction of desires or the immediate appeasement of suffering, an impulse natural in infancy. Every mother knows that the infant wants what he wants when he wants it. Growth to maturity requires that to a large measure this infantile impulse be given up; where this growth does not occur, the demands of real situations in adult life may create deep anxiety, for the self is so identified with its desires that failure to find immediate satisfaction is felt as a threat to its very existence.

To come back to Esau. He was hungry. He wanted the immediate satisfaction of his desire, the appeasement of his tensions. The food was available, but it was not his. How much would he give for it? Jacob asked a high price. Esau could have immediate satisfaction if he would part with his claim to the birthright—a claim which would be granted only later in life. Here anxiety arises in Esau, and it was the anxiety, not the hunger, which weakened him. "If I die, what good is this birthright?" Now one may live a long time in a state of hunger without dying; but a weak, immature person cannot long endure a strong state of anxiety. So Esau accepted immediate gratification. He demanded immediate gratification at the cost of a deeper satisfaction later. He remained immature.

In the New Testament there are a number of important references to anxiety. For one instance there is a clear description of unhealthy anxiety in the story of the visit of Jesus to Martha and Mary.[7] In this story we do not see the roots of anxiety, but rather one of the forms which it takes. It often drives a person into feverish activity which is far beyond the real demands of the life situation. The person cannot rest; rest is a state of relaxation which would bring the anxiety into consciousness and thereby create an awareness of the suffering which is being felt at deeper levels of the mind. If there is a feeling of guilt involved, as is usual, the feverish activity also becomes a means of self-punishment. The person feels that he has to justify himself by what he does. In some of his relationships the self is so threatened that he feels that he must bolster himself in all relationships by activity. His activity is an endeavor to secure the love of others, and like Martha, he becomes resentful if this love is not forthcoming. Sometimes he is a great asset around a church because he will take on so many services, but he finds little or no satisfaction in his activity. These persons literally believe in and practice the doctrine of salvation by good works. But this is a false doctrine both psychologically and religiously.

There is a need here to distinguish between healthy, wholesome work, and the kind of work illustrated by Martha. Healthy work is directed toward reasonable and worthy goals; it is a kind of investment of human energy which is necessary for health, and is a concrete expression of the positive faith and values to which one holds. It is an expression of love rather than a demand for love. Such work is emotionally and spiritually satisfying. Jesus himself was a worker, but not of the order of Martha.

Jesus handled this situation helpfully. He remained calm because of his own inner faith. Martha's anxiety did not make him anxious. This is a necessary attitude if one is to help an anxious person; one must be secure in his own values.

Jesus also had a deep understanding of both women. Undoubtedly more was said than is recorded in our Scriptures, but in what is recorded we see Jesus pointing calmly to a kind of relationship which creates trust and confidence. He did not give Martha four easy steps to overcome her anxiety; he suggested a deeper and more fundamental approach. The "good portion" to which Jesus refers is the acceptance of the relationship which Jesus was offering her and which she was avoiding through her own concern with activity.

One of the most frequently quoted Biblical passages is "The fear of the Lord is the beginning of wisdom; a good understanding have all those who practice it." [8] Some psychiatrists quote this verse in support of the idea that religion is a bad thing because it teaches people to have fear. But they misunderstand the meaning of the word as used here. The meaning in the Biblical text is not that of fear as we ordinarily use the word, but rather of awe and reverence.

Wisdom and understanding are gained as we approach life with awe and reverence. This attitude is found in the true scientist; he has a deep respect for the area of life from which he is trying to extract knowledge. Fear in the sense of danger which leads to fight or flight never produces wisdom either in the meaning of scientific knowledge or in the Biblical meaning of a practical understanding of life. The basic idea is expressed well in the book of Hebrews: "Let us offer to God acceptable worship, with reverence and awe." [9] Again, the writer of II Timothy is sure that the God of the Christian experience does not create fear in men: "for God did not give us a spirit of timidity but a spirit of power and love and self-control." [10]

There is another passage which is usually translated with the word "fear" to which some attention should be given. "There is no fear in love, but perfect love casts out fear. For fear has to do with punishment, and he who fears is not perfected in love." [11] To the extent that one does not feel loved, he will fear isolation or rejection for being sinful, as if there must be something wrong with him or he would be loved. He does not see that failure to be loved may be something of a failure of the other person in the relationship. Here John is assuring his readers that God does not fail in this way; that God loves men even though they may feel isolated from him; that when they come into a full realization of his love they will no longer fear because they will no longer feel isolated. They may suffer the natural consequences of their behavior, but there will not be punishment in the sense of isolation or rejection. Even a child can accept some punishment from a parent when he knows he is deeply loved; what is intolerable for the child is the feeling that he is not loved. Love casts out fear because it creates a relationship of trust or faith through which one feels accepted and hence forgiven.

In another passage Jesus tells his disciples that they are being sent out as sheep in the midst of wolves, so they are to be wise as serpents and harmless as doves.[12] When they are dragged into court they are not to be anxious as to what to say, for they will be given what to say. Here their relationship with God will provide courage which will free them to speak what is needful. Then follows a rather fearful picture, fearful on one side, but with a strong assurance of

strength on the other. There is nothing really to fear in the worst
that the enemies of the Gospel can do, provided, of course, that one
has the real security of the Gospel within himself. This is the
security of belonging to a community in which one is valued for
himself and therefore has the strength to serve or give value to the
community. Then comes the crucial thought: "Do not fear those
who kill the body but cannot kill the soul; rather fear him who can
destroy both soul and body in hell. . . . Fear not, therefore; you
are of more value than many sparrows."

The implication of these words is that there is something in life
which can actually threaten extinction, and that one needs to be
aware of this fact. This is the extinction of the self or soul by a
profound sense of worthlessness. The enemies of the Gospel can
persecute the Christians, but in persecution Christians have a sense
of strength in their solidarity, in their relation to one another, and
to Christ. Such solidarity gives courage. Beyond this there is the
deeper experience of realizing that they are of value to God as
persons. Such realization leads to grateful acknowledgment of the
relationship in which they feel valued and hence strengthened.

*The Bible and Faith*

There are many passages in the Bible where faith means a deep
trust, a confidence in another person or in God, a sense of the
reliability and dependability of God. Such experiences of faith lead
to certain qualities of mind and spirit, a sense of inner strength, a
genuine reassurance, a calmness, an inner peace, an awareness of
forgiveness, a consciousness of being whole, a certainty of knowledge
of God.[13] In the Bible faith is not primarily a set of beliefs, though
faith always has intellectual content. It is an emotional and spiritual
orientation to life and to God. It is a way of understanding and of
relating oneself to God, grounded in the insight that God relates
himself to man through redeeming love which requires a response
of love from man. Such a response heals the sense of separation as
experienced in anxiety, and becomes a motivating force for genuine
Christian living.

The eleventh chapter of the Epistle to the Hebrews sings to the glory of men and women of faith. But genuine faith is not always dramatic, and many stories of dramatic faith are found, upon close examination, not to be genuine. We see faith expressed in the experience of a frightened child's becoming quiet, losing its fear, and gaining strength to endure its pain in the presence of a strong, loving adult. We see it in a patient to whom a pastoral ministry brings a sense of eternal worth in the sight of God so that he can accept an operation quietly and courageously whatever the ultimate outcome may be. We also see it in a father who finds strength to do a high level of intellectual work while facing a long and severe illness in one of his children, and in a patient who recovers from an illness in spite of pessimistic predictions because he finds strength in the belief that there was still a work for him to do. A child's faith is an experience of outgoing trust in the benevolent reliability of the one in whom he believes. This same quality is present in mature faith, with the addition of an intellectual dimension through which the basis for faith is formulated. It is a profound, spontaneous experience, which cannot be created by an act of will, but often leaves the impression that it is given to one. It is always a response to a relationship in which a deep sense of belonging is realized, and a desire to give of oneself is created. In a sense, faith is a way of knowledge since it is always grounded in insight through which the person comes to understand trustworthy qualities in his relationships. Such insight is not produced, but may be supported, by reason.

It is such an experience of faith that Jesus describes in the Sermon on the Mount.[14] Jesus did not advise—"don't be anxious"—and stop there. As is clear in other passages, he knew that with certain orientations, or certain relationships, people would be anxious. He understood that under some circumstances everyone would feel anxious. But he also knew a different experience, one which realized God as utterly dependable and reliable, so that a man could make a positive response enabling him also to become dependable and reliable. It was a relationship through which one could discover aspects of himself that he could trust and use, binding up his needs and ambitions in one great endeavor, the kingdom of God and his righteousness.

The Gospels describe two experiences of Jesus which test this attitude of faith. One was the temptation.[15] Here are three problems which every man meets, and the outcome depends on whether his basic attitude is one of faith or one of anxiety. First the problem of satisfying human needs, one's own needs, especially when there has been a prolonged denial. Here is a repetition of the problem of Esau. The point of the experience is not that needs should not be satisfied, but that they should be met within the orientation of faith that includes the entire Word of God. Jesus, experiencing but not driven by anxiety, was able to deny himself immediate gratification when by so doing he would rob himself of a greater future satisfaction. He could endure present tension for the sake of a larger future goal. In so doing he could accept and participate in the Word of God as he saw it revealed in himself and in the spiritual documents of his own day. Understanding such a solution is difficult for one who insists on immediate gratification regardless of future consequences.

We cannot intellectualize ourselves into this emotional and spiritual orientation. We can only understand that man does not live by bread alone when we have been given something more than bread, that is, love, along with and in addition to bread. The overemphasis on material values is often an attempt to satisfy frustrated emotional and spiritual needs. Jesus, in this temptation, emphasizes the wholeness of life and the relation of God's redemptive process to wholeness. Overemphasis on the physical or material values is a form of illness: a symptom of the failure to achieve wholeness.

In the second temptation, Jesus met another common human problem, that of outgrowing our infantile sense of omnipotence which leads us, as adults, to play God, or to confuse our inner impulses with the voice of God. Or to put it differently, the problem of accepting reality as it is and relating to it, rather than following a childish fantasy of ourselves that implies our superiority to reality. Still a little differently, it is the problem of conforming our childish wishes to reality, so that they become mature, or distorting reality by insisting that it conform to our wishes. This is the temptation which Eve faced; she felt that she could distort reality and that reality would then conform to her distortion. But the price we pay for distorting reality, either immediate or ultimate reality, is the sacrifice of our own health and wholeness.

Here again we see Jesus expressing his faith. God, and the order of nature which God had created, is dependable and reliable. The full satisfaction of inner needs and the fulfillment of oneself comes not through forcing one's childish sense of omnipotence on to life, but by bringing one's wishes into harmony with reality. Even before the scientific formulation of the law of gravity, men knew that jumping off the pinnacle of the temple would cause injury or death. But there is a childish wish in man to deny such reality and to place the responsibility on God. Surely, if God loves us he will not let us hurt ourselves! The insight of Jesus here is that each person must accept responsibility for himself, not expect God to take it for him. Faith in the dependability of God gives strength to take responsibility for the conduct of one's own life and the solution of one's own problems. And it teaches one not to hide behind a false or immature sense of righteousness, but to be honest about those attitudes through which he is harming himself.

Again Jesus faced another common perplexity in the orientation of faith—the problem of power. Anxiety drives men to seek power over others. This was the Tempter's idea. All the kingdoms of the world and the glory of them! What power! But faith sees all problems in the light of God's love and dependability and care, not only for oneself but for all men alike. In this situation the response of faith is not one of power over others, but power to serve others; not a doing to others but a being something to others. Faith offers a relationship through which we give to others the security which releases their isolation and anxiety, and makes a sense of fellowship possible.

In relating these experiences the Bible uses the word "Tempter." What does this word mean? From the psychological point of view, there is never a temptation without anxiety. The crux of the problem of temptation is dealing with the anxiety involved in the conflicting possibilities. It is anxiety that leads men to sacrifice important and real future goals for immediate satisfactions, to try to force reality to conform to their wishes, and to seek power over others. The Biblical story seems to personify anxiety as the "Tempter." The significant aspect of this experience of Jesus is that he experienced profound anxiety, but was able to master it through a faith that overcame the anxiety and gave a basis for a creative solution of the conflict. This is a great spiritual achievement and has a profound influence on mental and physical health. But such faith is always the outgrowth of a dependable relationship with another, with man or God, or both.

It is significant that worship is involved in this temptation. Worship and service are related; one follows the other. This is true when worship proceeds from and in turn re-creates the experience of faith; the certainty that God is reliable, dependable, trustworthy. The kind of worship that is grounded in anxiety, that is, the temptation to worship Satan, is likely to intensify the anxiety, and to strengthen the need to have power over people.

Another experience recorded in the Gospels which deeply tests Jesus' orientation of faith is the story of Gethsemane,[16] a story which leaves no doubt about the presence of anxiety. Jesus is described as being very sorrowful and sore troubled. "His sweat became like great drops of blood falling down upon the ground." Sweating is a common physiological manifestation of anxiety. In daily parlance we speak of "sweating out" a bad experience. Jesus was facing a definite threat to himself. But faith controlled his decision! There was no neurotic escape here, but a facing of issues even though acceptance meant severe pain and death. The suffering was not desired nor enjoyed, as some neurotic persons enjoy suffering, but was unavoidable if the major goal was to be achieved. "The joy that was set before him," the great work of revealing the full love of God to man, made it both necessary and possible to accept present suffering and death. In such a decision there was a profound sense of the goodness, reliability and trustworthiness of God. The conflict in Gethsemane was Jesus' struggle to maintain this orientation in the face of the greatest threat that he had yet experienced.

Faith, in the sense of trust, is necessary for living on the basis of what the psychiatrist calls the reality principle, or what the Chris-

tian may call the will of God. Trust is necessary because the pressure of our inner desires makes us feel that any postponement or
frustration of satisfaction works against our welfare. Only in trust
can we see ahead of the present moment, and such trust grows only
through repeated experiences with significant persons who do not
let us down when we seek to renounce immediate pleasures for the
sake of a larger good. As one comes to trust persons in this sense he
becomes able also to trust God, for we know God largely through
persons. Christ's profound sense of trust can become for us a living
example with which we can identify, and thus find help in our
struggle to trust. This is one of the meanings of being Christlike.

This is the clear testimony of the Biblical writers. "Have no anxiety about anything, but in everything by prayer and supplication
with thanksgiving let your requests be made known to God. And
the peace of God, which passes all understanding, will keep your
hearts and your minds in Christ Jesus." [17] "Thou dost keep him in
perfect peace whose mind is stayed on thee." [18] "Now faith is the
assurance of things hoped for, the conviction of things not seen." [19]
Each of these passages has carried a wealth of meaning to Christians. In various ways they indicate the inner strength, the calmness,
the peace which are the products of a response of trust to the
dependability and reliability of God. It is not an easy peace of mind,
nor a superficial peace of soul that comes by outward conformity.
It is rather the peace of God. It is nothing which man creates for
himself; it is the product of a trusting relationship with God. It
becomes the basis of hope for the future, the ground for believing
in possibilities which are not yet actualities; a preview of what is
possible on the basis of what is actual. Thus a child who has experienced tender love will be able to have faith in its continuance; a
child who has never experienced this love will have difficulty in
having such faith. Faith grounded in love has a profound effect on
both mental and physical health, since it provides the basis for a
harmonious functioning of the whole person in all of his relationships, and makes possible the achievement of those values on which
the well-being of the person and of the group depends.

In summary then, faith is a basic orientation that involves emotional acceptance of, and response to, a person whom one knows as dependable, reliable and trustworthy. It is a taking into oneself of the love which is given by the object of faith, whether that object be another human being or God. Love is important here since it is only love that is ultimately trustworthy in personal relationships. In the New Testament, faith is a response to love, a response of loyalty and devotion. Faith is grounded in insight into those aspects of our relationships which, being trustworthy, give a basis for strength and stability. Such insight is never logical proof, but a see-ing, a sensing, a feeling that is clear enough to become a basis of personal response and action. Faith enables us—sets us free—to use our energies and abilities in real ways rather than in distorted defenses against anxiety.

There is a profound insight in the New Testament that faith makes men whole.[20] The Revised Standard Version of the New Testament uses the word "well," an apt translation since wholeness means health. Faith creates a strength which makes possible the constant facing, understanding and resolution of experiences which create anxiety. In doing this, faith functions in the direction of health or wholeness.

Wholeness and faith may be seen from another perspective, that of conscious self-direction rather than blind, impulsive living. But conscious self-direction requires strength to evaluate situations and relationships for what they are, strength to understand inner needs and desires for what they are and direct them toward satisfying and creative ends, strength to master external circumstances which are obstacles, strength to give our energy in useful work and our love to our fellow men. Such strength is the utilization of latent poten-tiality. The strong person utilizes inner potentiality of which the anxious person cannot be aware, and certainly cannot use. Just as the nervous system binds various organs of the body together in a whole, so faith binds energies together toward conscious, self-directed goals of love and work. Work, for the sick patient, is doing that which is necessary for the mastery of the illness.

Pastoral counseling offers illustrations of what is meant by whole-ness. A young woman had developed an attitude in which the question, "What do I get out of it?" was prominent in her relationships with others. She was always scheming to exploit others, and felt hurt when her efforts were rebuffed. Her impulse then was to hurt the other person. Behind this reaction was a great deal of anxiety growing out of childhood relationships.

As she worked through her experiences to the place where she could see this pattern of exploitation and the anxieties out of which it grew, she came to understand and release these attitudes and also the hostility which was rooted in them. This led her to a different quality of relationship with others. In her own words, "Now I can be myself. And being myself sometimes means just listening to people without reacting one way or the other. There is no need to react as they are not going to hurt me, and I no longer need to hurt them. I seem to have a new confidence in myself and also in other people. I don't always have to tell others what to do or get them to tell me what to do. Many of these things that used to be problems are not problems now. Many situations are the same, but I feel strong enough now to take them in my stride. The word which comes to me to describe this new feeling is 'whole.' I feel whole instead of being pulled apart."

Our problem then becomes that of the development of faith and the cure of anxiety. It should be obvious by now that this is not just an intellectual process. One cannot think himself into a faith that makes for wholeness, but thinking may help. Neither is faith achieved by a magical act. God does not remove anxiety by sleight of hand. The human wish for this is understandable as the remains of a childish wish for protection and care. But life in maturity is not like that, nor is God a cosmic baby sitter. The God of Jesus rather offers men a fellowship which involves a response of using all the powers that they have to deal with anxiety. One of the great temptations of the Church today is to give men easy answers, for this is what many ask.

Sometimes adults experience obstacles to a response of faith in God that are related to earlier experiences with other persons. The capacity to make a response of faith is first expressed when the infant feels a warmth, tenderness and love from its mother when it is being fed. If it feels a threat, a rejection, a coldness in its mother it will respond with anxiety. It is here, long before the child can understand words, that the first lessons of faith may be learned, and if the child does not learn a basic trust at this early stage it may be difficult for him ever to learn it. As a child grows he has many experiences with people who show themselves to be trustworthy or untrustworthy. Sooner or later he will learn that his parents are not completely trustworthy, and that no human being is completely so. He will have to learn to discern between that which is trustworthy in others and in himself, and that which is not. It is particularly important that persons who represent the Church or religion to the child do not let him down. Most skepticism about religion is grounded in experiences of being hurt by people who profess to be religious.

Here is the significance of the life and revelation of Christ. It is difficult for many to experience faith in God directly; God is vague, far away, or perhaps threatening and punishing. God may be too closely identified with an untrustworthy parent or other person. But Jesus as the revelation of God gives us an objective, concrete picture of the reality of God. Basic in this revelation is the kind of love which is trustworthy, which begets faith. To the extent that our orientation is controlled by anxiety, it will be difficult to make a response of faith to what we see in Christ. Such a response may first involve deep changes in which attitudes or relationships which create anxiety are worked through gradually and given up. This is one reason why so many people find difficulty in becoming and continuing as Christians in a vital sense. Peter and Paul had their problems, but gradually and painfully worked through them. Judas failed to work through the problems involved in making a response of faith, loyalty, and devotion to Jesus.

It is at this point that the fellowship of the Church has a real opportunity and responsibility. For the pastor, there is a tremendous opportunity to bring to men, not verbally, but through his life, a sense of the trustworthiness of God. There is also the opportunity, for which he needs much more training than he usually receives in theological school, to help persons who find themselves in this anxiety-faith conflict. In the fellowship of the Church there is again the opportunity to give experiences that are trustworthy and loving, and which mediate the trustworthiness and love of God. The task of the Church is to show forth the love of God so that men may see and grow in their trust.

It may come as a hard saying, but there are persons whose anxiety is so deep that they will never be able to develop faith strong enough to give them stability without some form of direct help. Some may be helped by a pastor who has adequate understanding, experience and training. Others are in need of treatment by a psychotherapist, which is both more intensive and extensive than the pastor can give. It could well be that at the conclusion of such treatment, there will be a need for the aid of a pastor in developing a positive religious faith. Most psychotherapists do not believe that it is their task to lead their patients into a specifically Christian view of life.

One of the requirements for any process of therapy is that of a certain minimum faith in the helper as a person. In this connection even Jesus felt himself limited in giving help; he could help only those who had faith in him.[21]

Apart from faith in the helper there is another problem. There is a profound need for honesty at the foundation of human life, an honesty which religious people often try to circumvent by easy answers. Elimination of anxiety occurs as we are able to relate the anxiety to the relationships out of which it grew. This means a genuine honesty about how we feel and why we feel that way. Self-deception—saying that we do not feel anxious when we do, or that we are anxious about a certain experience when it is really something else that we are anxious about—self-deception is the basis of much illness and also of much distorted religion. Any religious cure of anxiety which is not grounded on genuine honesty with ourselves is bound to do harm. But such honesty is always the fruit of a relationship with a person or group in which we find acceptance and understanding which makes self-honesty and self-acceptance possible.

The emphasis on the relation of faith to wholeness and health leads to the question of faith healing. Some so-called faith cures would be ludicrous if they were not so tragic. When a child is allowed to die because his parents refuse medical care on grounds of religious faith we have a tragic denial of the basic meaning of Christian love. For a person to refuse medical treatment for himself on similar grounds is to tempt God to make him a special case. For a person to claim a faith cure for a nondiagnosed or improperly diagnosed illness claimed to be cancer, is exploitation of religious faith. These things all Christian churches ought to disavow.

To understand what may happen in "faith cures" one must understand the close relation of physical, emotional and spiritual processes, and that experiences on one level have a marked influence on all levels. A similar understanding is needed of the close relationship existing between the organism and the environment, in which each is constantly being influenced by and reacting to the other. Since many physical illnesses are either caused by or complicated by such feelings as anxiety, guilt and hostility, the symptoms of such illnesses may be removed, and the affected organ may return to normal functioning through resolution of the conflict. At other times the symptom has brought certain physical changes so that the organ involved cannot return to its normal functioning even though tension is relieved.

There is no doubt that many so-called faith cures are experienced by persons suffering from emotionally produced illnesses through relationships and processes which we understand today. Some persons are very suggestible and through the proper rituals and ceremonies can find symptoms relieved, but only to find other symptoms developing later, because the underlying cause is not removed. Other illnesses, created by a desire to get out of an intolerable situation, clear up miraculously when the situation is changed. However, the patient may not understand what has taken place and under certain influences may claim a faith cure.

On the other hand, there is much about the nature of illness and the experience of healing which is not understood today from either a medical or a religious point of view. When we know that in any healing the faith of the patient in the healer is of profound significance, we cannot deny the possibility of the significance of faith in ways we do not yet understand.

An illustration of a relief from symptoms which was accepted by the patient as a faith cure is the case of a man of about middle age who had a heart attack. Although his wife belonged to a religious group which does not believe in medical care, he insisted on being sent to the hospital. There a specialist in heart diseases examined him, laughed and walked out of the room. The specialist evidently discovered that the man's heart was in good condition, saw beneath to the unconscious self-deception which was taking place, but became irritated by this aspect of the man's illness. The patient himself became very angry at the physician. The next day a representative of his wife's religious group was brought in, and the patient was "healed" of his heart attack, that is, his symptoms were removed by "faith." Now, convinced he had had a bona fide heart attack, extremely angry at a representative of the medical profession, convinced he was cured by a representative of his wife's religious group, he surrendered to his wife's pressure of twenty years and joined the group. But having made his decision under the constant pressure from his wife, augmented now by a supposed illness, he developed resentments toward her religious group. Five years later these produced new physical symptoms, such as severe pains in the back, and an almost uncontrollable impulse to disrupt a religious service by jumping through a window of the church.

This man illustrates something very important to our problem. Any sick person will feel dependent. Some rebel against this dependency and do not want anyone to do for them. Others accept their dependency and want to lean heavily on a stronger person, sometimes too heavily, identifying themselves with this stronger person and taking strength from him. This patient was rebelling against pressures from his wife and a need within himself to be dependent on her, or as he said, "to be in harmony with her." The experience which he interpreted as a heart attack gave him the need to depend on and identify with a strong man, the physician. But the physician rejected him, and there was nothing left to do but accept dependency on his wife and her group.

Illness heightens normal dependency needs and may grow out of dependency needs. When a person has suffered deeply, when he feels he cannot go on any longer, yet he cannot give up in death, he may come to the place where he surrenders his resistance to dependency and accepts such a relationship with a stronger person, perhaps a relative or friend, a physician, Christ, God, the Church or another group. Responsibility is assumed by these persons or groups, or so it is felt by the sick individual. But a dependent person is likely to seek control of the one on whom he is dependent, saying in effect, if you do not do thus and so for me, I will become ill again. It is possible for a doctor or religious leader to foster such dependency without realizing what is taking place. This is a strong factor in most, if not all, "faith cures." Here dependency is confused with faith. To be sure, there is a certain kind of dependency in all faith; but real faith has other qualities which make a vast difference!

One of these differences concerns the object of our faith. Is the one in whom we have faith worthy of that faith? It is the insight of the Bible that the object which is ultimately worthy of our faith is God as revealed in Christ. This God manifests himself within human relationships in terms of self-giving, redemptive love. The response of faith in such a God requires that we face those aspects of our life which prevent the full realization of our potentiality for love. In this very act we move away from self-deception to self-honesty, from illness toward wholeness. A real experience of faith always brings insight into some aspect of our own being, since it asks us to respond in a manner which is appropriate to that object.

Another difference between dependency and faith is in the nature and outcome of faith. In the New Testament faith always involves a dependency on God as the source and sustainer of life. But it is also grounded in the insight that we have freedom and responsibility; the insight that our life is in our hands to make of it what we can. The final question concerns what we have done with that which has been given to us. This insight into freedom and responsibility requires strength to meet our own problems. It breaks with the childish kind of dependency which says that it is up to God to cure us and to solve our problems. To be healthy we must utilize all of our powers and capacities, but always with the consciousness that these are ultimately gifts from God. We cannot do less and be Christian.

In considering the relation of faith to cure, the difference between illness and disease should be kept in mind. Illness is the experience of a person, and as such it usually involves every aspect of his being, physical, emotional, social and spiritual. Disease is a process which takes place within the organism. Tuberculosis, polio, schizophrenia are disease processes. In every experience of illness there is anxiety, since illness is a threat to the whole man. In every cure faith plays a part, though the part may be different in different persons. In a sense every disease is an anxiety disease and every cure is a faith cure. In what is perhaps the most normal abnormality, childbirth, anxiety is present, but a woman's faith in her own physical processes and in her physician can make the difference between panic and confidence. It is false to think of faith as curing a disease process on the physiological level. Faith gives strength to deal with the process.

However, immature and helpless dependency may be gratified by another person, and thus a large element in an illness may be removed. Or a person may so identify with a religious object such as Christ or the Virgin Mary that his immature need for dependency is satisfied and he no longer needs to remain ill.

Many psychiatrists have commented on the speed with which an organ may return to proper functioning once an inner tension such as anxiety is relieved. But a person who undergoes this experience of immature faith healing will likely remain immature in his personal and religious relationships. He will have need to defend the kind of experience which cured him of his illness, and one way of defending it is by insisting that others follow the same practice. If his dependent relationship is threatened in any way, such as his religion being questioned, he may become ill again. Such immature faith may have personal value, and may be preferred to a diet of drugs and sleeping pills, but it should not be confused with mature faith in the New Testament sense.

Faith, in the New Testament sense, is a response to a God whom one experiences as loving and accepting, but a response which calls out our deepest strength. At times this strength may be spent in strenuous effort; at times it means deep relaxation. But it is not a self-produced relaxation, it is rather a deep calmness growing out of the realization that one has nothing to fear. Such strength can muster the resources of a person to fight a disease process which is operating within him. Whether this leads to cure will depend also on the nature and extent of the process, on the medical treatment available and effective in reversing the process, and on other factors. But a person of real faith does not demand cure as a price for his faith. He can accept less, if this is what the realities of the case demand, and like Paul [22] find strength through his faith to live with a thorn in the flesh. Or, if death is to be the outcome, he can accept this with serenity and peace. Through his faith in the ultimate goodness and love of God as the source of life he overcomes any fear that death itself brings. This person is at the opposite extreme from the patient who has a wish to die because he is afraid to live. The man of mature faith is able to accept either life or death because he has lost his fear of both.

Faith is always a response to something which presents itself as trustworthy, while anxiety is a response to something which we feel as a threat. Men of faith have always accepted their experience of faith as a gift. The Bible uses the word "grace" for this experience of receiving from God love which makes faith possible. "For by grace you have been saved through faith; and this is not your own doing, it is the gift of God." [23] It is God's acceptance of us that makes it possible to accept ourselves and to discover who we are in relationship to him and to our fellow men. Rather than a frantic attempt to develop faith and get rid of anxiety by various self-hypnotic methods which are being advocated today, it would be much better to center our attention on the grace of God as revealed in the daily contact of Jesus with human beings. Faith might then come. This is indeed the experience of redemption, this regaining of trust, and it comes to one as a miracle of grace.

## Chapter Three

# Guilt and Forgiveness

THROUGHOUT the long history of mankind, sin and guilt have been considered as causative factors in illness. Jesus very clearly illustrates this view when he approaches the paralytic with the statement, "My son, your sins are forgiven." [1] Apparently in this situation Jesus felt that this man's major problem was guilt, and that this would have to be eliminated before physical cure could take place.

This insight of Jesus has been confirmed by modern medicine. Physicians have discovered that guilt, like anxiety, may serve to inhibit or paralyze the functions of the body or mind, or the same feelings may serve to overstimulate these functions. Either paralysis or overactivity in any of its various forms produces symptoms of illness.

A young woman had been going to a physician for a number of months receiving treatment for an upset stomach, lack of appetite and serious loss of weight. Sensing that something was on her mind, the physician finally sent her to a minister who had some skill in dealing with spiritual problems. The girl wanted to talk, though talking was painful. She had a burden of guilt growing out of family relationships and out of sexual activities. These guilt feelings were finding expression through her digestive processes; she literally had more than she could "stomach." She welcomed the first interview as an opportunity to throw off some of the intense feeling and to share her situation for the first time with another human being. She felt it was a miracle that immediately after this interview her digestive processes began to function properly. But this was no miracle in the strict meaning of that word. What had happened to her was well understood by the pastor. However, the whole problem was not ended there; it took some months of patient and sometimes painful work before a permanent solution was reached. The process was not primarily one of solving a problem, but rather of helping her grow so that she could work out a new pattern of living on the basis of more mature motives.

Any psychiatrist, pastoral counselor, or observant physician could multiply illustrations of the way in which feelings of guilt contribute to organic illnesses, to mental illnesses, or to criminal behavior. A common question is, How do guilt feelings begin? Where do we first learn to feel guilty?

Some students of human nature believe that guilt may be produced in early infancy. An infant who feels unloved and rejected will also feel worthless and hence guilty. Some parents begin to punish infants very early for acts which displease them. One authority believes that the first severe sense of guilt arises in many infants when, having grown some teeth, they bite their mother's breast. This bite is very painful, and the mother instinctively reacts with a slap or at least with a quick withdrawal of the breast. Such an experience of pain and loss is frightening to the child. It serves to inhibit the impulse to bite, but the mother may notice that the infant develops some new behavior of a destructive kind, also perhaps involving the mouth. The impulse which is forbidden expression in one way seeks other ways which will not be so frightening.

Guilt often arises at the stage of weaning or toilet training. Suddenly the child may be made to feel that his customary behavior is wrong; he is supposed to take up new ways. He is much more likely to feel guilty about these processes if his mother and others caring for him do not show a genuine warm love and understanding for him. Harshness, condemnation, punishment, scoldings, withdrawal from the child, create feelings of guilt and leave the child mystified as to why he should be so uncomfortable. Severity in toilet training may make the child feel guilty about his body and bodily functions. This guilt may later be related to the sexual organs, and the child may feel guilty because he is a sexual being.

Feelings of guilt may be further developed as the child continues to grow. His show of affection to one parent may be felt to be disapproved by the other parent; indeed, sometimes it is openly disapproved. A simple question about where babies come from, or some other question dealing with sex, may be handled in a way that tells him that his question is considered wrong. In many other kinds of everyday experiences adults may indicate disapproval of the child's feelings or behavior. Sometimes rather intense guilt feelings are developed around a specific incident. At other times such feelings are generalized through a rather constant attitude shown to the child, so that he comes to feel guilty not only about acts, but also about feelings. An extreme example was a little boy who developed the feeling that it was wrong to want anything, so that when he became aware of any desire, he also became aware of a feeling of guilt.

Guilt feelings are associated with the conscience. In early childhood, conscience is developed almost entirely through the feelings. Because of the approval or disapproval of others, the child feels that a given act or desire is right or wrong. The child has not reached a state of development where he can weigh matters for himself; he must accept the authority of others. This is imperative because he is likely to suffer if he goes contrary to the wishes of others. So in childhood conscience begins on the basis of feelings and on a pattern similar to that held by those in authority. This kind of conscience may not be very constructive in adult life.

There is another aspect of conscience that anxious, guilt-laden people find difficult to understand. A child may learn right from wrong, not only through punishment, but more constructively through love and understanding. This kind of conscience is not grounded in feelings of guilt but in a desire to be like the loving and loved parent. This kind of conscience will be more positive and constructive than a guilt-laden conscience. Kindness shown by the parent will help the child want to be kind. There is incongruity in trying to teach a child to be kind by punishing him for being unkind. Punishment may or may not deter unkind acts; it can never teach the child to be kind.

One of the profound emotional and spiritual needs of human beings is for a sense of togetherness or belonging. A feeling of isolation is hard to endure, especially for children. Since we all have this need for togetherness, we help each other in a relationship of mutual acceptance. Also we tend to create relationships which give others feelings similar to ours. Adults who feel isolated are likely to treat children in a way that makes them feel isolated; such children will feel anxiety and guilt and will show this in their behavior. Thus separation, anxiety and feelings of guilt are very closely related. It is through a relationship of love, acceptance and understanding that separation is removed, belongingness is established, and growth is promoted. Conscience grounded in love for self and others, love that seeks both our own and our neighbor's good in mutual relationships, becomes a means of positive growth; conscience grounded in fear of separation and punishment tends to restrict the personality so that it can be neither healthy nor Christian.

An illustration of the way in which patterns of guilt feelings set up in childhood may endure into adult life is a man of about forty years of age, reared by a very severe father in whose eyes the boy found no approval or acceptance. As a man he is successful in his professional life, but he has a problem in his family life. As a Christian he believes that he should be able to show much more love than he is able to show to his family. By nature also he is capable of deep feelings of warmth and affection, but he feels too guilty and fearful to give these feelings expression. Such feelings of affection, it appears, were particularly disapproved by his father; he was made to feel guilty about them, and even as an adult his guilt is so strong that his feelings of love must be repressed. It is easy to say that since he has become a man he should put away this childish guilt. But many times we do not understand just what is involved in putting away childish guilt; it is an achievement sometimes very difficult to accomplish.

The way in which we deal with feelings of guilt in ourselves depends on several closely related factors. These are the strength of the feelings of guilt as compared with the strength of the self to face and deal with those feelings. A little child has not had time nor experience to develop much inner strength, so that a small measure of guilt feelings may be intolerable. An adult who has not gained much inner strength may also find a rather small measure of guilt feelings intolerable or may be unable to prevent guilt feelings from accumulating and intensifying. An adult who has inner strength may meet guilt-producing experiences of rather severe magnitude and still face and handle them constructively. How do guilt feelings make us sick? Certain answers can be suggested.

Because feelings of guilt are so painful, and because they are often too strong for an individual to face and handle openly, they are pushed back to deeper levels of the mind. Technically this is called repression. Repression is a protective process of the mind which makes one unaware of feelings that are painful. One may not be aware of guilt feelings, but unconsciously may feel very guilty. If this is the case, the feelings of guilt will find some disguised form of expression, such as a symptom of physical illness, or a compulsive need to wash his hands or engage in some other unexplainable activity, or the idea that others are watching him. These symptoms serve as a defense against allowing the feeling of guilt to become conscious again. This is where the illness comes in. The person finds himself forced by feelings of which he is not aware to act or think in certain ways that produce unhappiness and destroy his capacity for effective living. He is sick because he does not consciously know what makes him do what he consciously does not want to do, and because he cannot control his behavior. Part of him is controlling all of him.

Some forms of physical illness, as in the case of the young woman with the digestive problem discussed earlier, are expressions of guilt. Guilt sets up tension which may affect any organ of the body, particularly one which in some way symbolizes the nature of the problem. The stomach and digestive system often serve to express conflicts in the area of love and sex. The symptoms, which are painful, also serve the purpose of self-punishment. Punishment temporarily allays, but does not eliminate, feelings of guilt. The punishment has to be repeated many times; the continuing symptom is a continuing punishment. Of course, the person is not aware that he is punishing himself. Becoming aware of the feelings behind the symptoms is one of the steps in removing the symptom, and with many persons this requires treatment.

Another form of defense against guilt feelings is some form of unreasonable inhibition which leads to failure. A student may be so inhibited in his study by guilt feelings that he fails. The failure also serves as self-punishment. Men and women fail in many aspects of life because of feelings of guilt which prohibit their success. Others are driven into overactivity by feelings of guilt. They have to prove that they are good, capable, successful or strong. This apparent strength compensates for their guilt. At the same time the intense drive into activity coupled with extreme denial of many other desires becomes a form of self-punishment.

Another form of unhealthy defense against guilt feelings is a sense of self-righteousness. The feeling that we are or must be perfect, that we are always and completely right while others are always and completely wrong, the holier-than-thou attitudes found in some religious persons and groups, are defenses against repressed guilt. Feeling superior to others prevents feelings of guilt or failure from reaching consciousness. Such a reaction usually has a mixture of hostility in that the individual feels it necessary to attack those who do not share his opinions, sometimes rather violently. Such attacks may be rationalized in the name of truth, but actually they are inspired by hostility and guilt. This person is very likely to be harsh and legalistic in his judgments.

Another expression of repressed guilt lies in what is often called an oversensitive conscience. The person who feels that others are always criticizing him, who takes uncritical comments as criticism, who feels that others know that he has done something wrong when they do not have the slightest knowledge of his behavior—such persons are struggling with their own guilt feelings which they project on others. Unable to face their feelings honestly, it seems that others are accusing them falsely. Such ideas sometimes develop to extreme forms which indicate severe mental illness.

Another kind of expression of repressed guilt is seen in the person whose guilt feelings, developed in human relationships in childhood, are projected onto God. Such persons have a feeling that God is condemning and punishing them. They may feel that physical illness is punishment for their sins, though intellectually they find it hard to believe in such a God. Others find that their guilt interferes with faith in God or any kind of close relationship to God. This is especially likely to be the case when in childhood pastors and teachers of religion present a kind of theological and moral emphasis that reinforces condemning parental and community attitudes, so that God becomes identified with a punishing, rather than with a loving, adult. Guilt may be so built into the structure of religious feeling and ideas that it becomes the central motivating element in the individual's relation to God and in his religious thinking. This is both unhealthy and unchristian.

There is a relationship between our religious beliefs and our feelings. Feelings that are repressed unconsciously influence our view of ourself, of others and of God. Some persons have a strong need to intellectualize their feelings. This means the development of a system of ideas or beliefs which express in intellectual form the attitudes and feelings of which they are not fully aware. There are those who begin and end their view of man with the belief that he is depraved and sinful and powerless to take any responsibility for his condition. They may emphasize the wrath of God in the sense of irrational punishment. They see little if any good in man. His salvation must come by a miraculous intervention of God, on whom he must cast himself in a mood of utter worthlessness and dejection. Granting the main premise, such ideas may be developed logically, but the difficulty is that their basis is an emotional attitude of self-condemnation and guilt. Some persons who feel this way also feel a compulsion to force others to feel the same way. They cannot achieve a sense of togetherness in love; they achieve their solidarity in ideas of man's great sinfulness. Misery does love company.

Some methods of evangelism unconsciously aim at relating childhood guilt to God, and then seek to find release for the guilt in a conversion experience, which often results in further repression rather than release. For most of us childhood guilt is best released through a relationship with a person who in a measure represents a parent, but a good, loving parent, with whom we can talk about the feelings and the relationships out of which they grew. In this way we find it possible to give up childish feelings and develop more mature attitudes toward others and toward God.

Guilt has other harmful effects on the human mind and spirit. For example, a person may repress a feeling of guilt about a given act but still remember the act. He will then insist he does not feel guilty about such activity and continue it. Some repress their feelings of guilt about sexual activities, insisting that they have no guilt. But they continue to feel hostile to others, particularly to those who might find out about their sexual activities or who might show disapproval. This hostility is a disguised expression of guilt.

Other persons forget that they have had certain experiences but retain in consciousness a feeling of guilt. They may come to the pastor asking why they feel so guilty; they have done nothing to deserve the feeling. But being emotionally persuaded that they are guilty, they find some imaginary activity to which to attach their guilt, confessing a great feeling of guilt about some insignificant matter. Attaching guilt to the wrong object or circumstance, they are not brought to face the real cause, which would be very painful. This is another protective device.

Again a person may be unaware either of his feelings of guilt or of the reason for them, and hence does not realize the influence such feelings have on him. Or he may be aware of both feelings of guilt and the reason. This too is a painful situation, but essentially healthy, provided he proceeds to find adequate help in working out the feelings and in correcting the situation realistically.

Feelings of guilt indicate that something is wrong in an individual's relationships. It is the relationship that needs to be dealt with, not the guilt directly. Feelings of guilt tend to produce some symptoms of illness when they are more intense than a person can tolerate, when they are stronger than the situation creating them warrants, when they are created because of behavior which a person does not understand and cannot control, and when they are the result of condemnatory attitudes on the part of a stronger person, so that they lead to a sense of helplessness. Also strong feelings of guilt in adults which are the expression of childhood relationships are unhealthy.

On the other hand, there may be a beneficial aspect to feelings of guilt, if properly handled. Guilt grows out of faulty relationships and where it becomes a starting point for discovering and correcting such relationships it is used beneficially. In our culture, and in much of our church life, we have tended to use guilt as a means of control, or a basis for religious living, and in so doing have hurt many persons.

In some situations guilt is a very appropriate feeling. A person who commits murder should feel guilty and there is something deficient about him if he does not. A person who entertains murderous impulses needs to be aware of the seriousness of his feelings, and do something constructive about them before they result in action. Guilt feelings may or may not make control of such impulses possible, but in either case an unhealthy situation is produced. The healthy and constructive approach is to seek help to work out the hostile feelings so that love becomes a stronger motivation than hostility.

### Guilt and Forgiveness in the Bible

The Bible is very much concerned with sin, guilt and forgiveness. The opening pages attempt to account for sin, and to portray its meaning. The story of Adam and Eve does not explain sin and guilt; it simply and powerfully portrays the human situation. It re-enacts the experience of every child when he first suffers disapproval and punishment at the hands of a powerful parent. The story re-enacts the experience of every person who comes to the awareness that there is a Reality in life on whom he cannot force his will without being hurt. The positive side of this experience is the awareness that the discovery and acceptance of the nature of Reality gradually leads to the fulfillment of one's life.

The story of Adam and Eve has been traditionally called the story of the "Fall of Man." But it might be called the story of the "Dawn of Conscience," for it portrays man's dawning awareness of the difference between good and evil, right and wrong. There can be no conscience, no action or choice with the foreknowledge of consequences, without the awareness of "good" and "evil."

But what is "good" and "evil"? For the infant good is whatever satisfies his needs and gives him a comfortable feeling. Whatever is frustrating, anxiety-producing, or causes pain is evil. The infant has no other criterion by which to judge. In so far as an adult remains infantile or childish in his emotional development, he may live by the same criterion.

But the growing child learns that life has another side, and that action which results in a good feeling may also bring harmful results. He does not learn this lesson easily. It is a threat to his sense of omnipotence—his belief that he can control his world. It is also a threat to his kind of self-love which makes him feel that he should always be taken care of by some greater power, rather than accepting responsibility for himself and his own actions. No child accepts the fact that he cannot force his will on life without going through a stage of rebellion and hostility. This rebellion may be openly expressed as it was by Eve and the prodigal son. Or it may be dutifully repressed and submerged as in the elder brother, only to come out later in an attempt to control the father's relation with the younger brother. This rebellion in the face of reality that challenges infantile omnipotence is expressed by the idea that we want to be as God, we want to be in control of our world. It does involve a Fall— a fall from our childish sense of omnipotence, but it is a fall that is necessary for growth to a more mature level of life where we can relate ourselves to others, to "life," to reality, or to God on the basis of mutual love and co-operation. What is thus seen as a "fall" from one point of view is the beginning of real growth from another. Man can never get back to that childish state of omnipotence except through a mental illness in which omnipotence finds expression in a delusion. But he can go forward through the pain of renouncing infantile desires, and through love and work move toward the mature fulfillment of himself in a relationship of mutual belonging with others and with God. In place of the estrangement of rebellion which creates profound anxiety, there can be a sense of security grounded in acceptance and belonging. Such growth is achieved through the kind of experiences in which we gain insight into ourselves and others, into the nature of life, the nature and meaning of our relationships with others and with God, the source of our being.

The tragedy of life lies in the fact that man does not want to give up his infantilism and become mature. In theological terms, he does not want to give up his sin of desire for omnipotence in order to become a real person, a Son of God in a human brotherhood, the kingdom of God. Sin thus is not fundamentally an act; it is a relationship of estrangement and isolation caused by setting the individual will in opposition to the will of God. This possibility of isolation seems to be inherent in human life; it is a reality which the story of Adam and Eve portrays. The story appears to account for the pain and labor of life on the basis of man's guilt, but this is a doctrine which Jesus did not accept. The pain of suffering and toil which is intolerable is that which is experienced without the fellowship with others which gives it meaning. It is this fellowship which Jesus stresses. The solution of the problem of guilt is in the Gospel, in a God whose love reaches out to man even to the point of accepting the suffering caused by man's rebellion in order to break down that rebellion and estrangement and create Sonship. Sonship, not omnipotence, is the way to health and salvation.

There are numerous illustrations of the problem of sin in the Old Testament, always with the condition of estrangement in the background. Cain [2] felt the rejection of his offering and responded with murderous hate. The brothers of Joseph [3] felt the favoritism of their father for the younger brother, and responded with hostility.

The Old Testament seeks to handle the problem of sin in several ways. One is through the law. The great foundation of the law is the Ten Commandments, a series of prohibitions and commands designed to control attitudes as well as actions. Honoring father and mother and covetousness are attitudes; stealing and adultery are actions. But behind all of these commandments is the same need on the part of the individual; the need for community, a sense of belonging and togetherness which these various acts or attitudes destroy. The law is grounded in insight into man's need for constructive group relationships and it attempts to protect and foster the satisfaction of that need.

But the law is not adequate to this task, for we can live well within the law and yet feel isolated. The experience of belonging which is so essential to emotional and spiritual well-being cannot be legislated, nor can it be created by punishment for behavior which is prohibited. Either the sense of belonging is grounded in actual human relationships or it does not exist. Only as these relationships are the expression of love, understanding, acceptance, faith and other such positive attitudes is a sense of real togetherness created.

The law has a definite relation to health. Not only are many laws designed to protect health, but the way in which the law is taught and enforced has a particular significance for emotional and spiritual health.

This deeper application can be illustrated in child-parent relationships. To the little child, the parent stands in a very powerful, authoritative position. Yet the child has a deep need for security and a sense of belonging with the parent. The parent may be very stern, legalistic and given to punishment in his relationship to the child. Obviously this attitude will tend to destroy any deep sense of togetherness, calling forth instead a response of fear which produces an oversevere conscience. Or it may bring a response of rebellion which produces an ability to break the law without any feeling of guilt. Indeed, it may produce an uncontrollable compulsion to violate the law. In other words, the quality of the relationships through which law is taught and enforced has a definite influence on health.

To be sure, some law is necessary in child raising. It is harmful to a child to be allowed to hurt other children. The child finds a certain sense of security in a consistently arranged world where he knows certain things are expected of him and certain restrictions are placed on him. But actually the demands and restrictions that are dictated by the reality of human life are not great. The danger is that they be magnified in number and in seriousness by guilt-laden adults and that they be enforced with a severity which the child feels to be rejection.

It is only through loving relationships that a healthy, creative and Christian conscience can be developed. The child wants to be like the loving person who in turn becomes the loved person. Feeling others sensitive to his needs, the child develops sensitivity to the needs of others as he matures from childhood through adolescence into maturity.

There is another aspect of the law which applies to health, that is, the danger of the wholesome functions of the law being distorted by unhealthy compulsiveness in regard to the law. This compulsion occurs in both groups and individuals. It occurred in the people of Israel during Old Testament times. It involves the pyramiding of law upon law, the attempt to balance the exact measure of the seriousness of an act against an exact measure of punishment; the need to create rules for the management of the minute details of life and the placing of legal values far above human values. Saul of Tarsus was a glowing example of compulsive legalism—he felt compelled to persecute and kill those who were members of a new religious group which emphasized love rather than the law. Human values and human relationships were completely denied in a compulsive drive to maintain a legalistic religion and personality. Behind such a destructive compulsion there is always deep anxiety and guilt which finds both expression and further development in the legalistic attitude itself.

This kind of legalistic compulsiveness is common in many of our churches today, and is one of the symptoms of the sickness of some of our religion. The individual or group says in effect, "You must accept this particular formula or you cannot be saved. It is this way and no other. You must do these particular things in this manner and with this frequency, or you cannot be saved." The particular formula and the particular actions will differ from person to person and group to group, but the principle is the same. The compulsive person must force himself and others into a fixed and rigid groove, and in religion he will justify this compulsion with the idea that his groove is the sole road to salvation. Behind this compulsiveness there is sometimes an intense energy which is indicative of the depth of the illness, but which may also carry a given idea or practice into large organizational expression.

Jesus had to face this kind of religion. He did so with a very creative attitude. He had come to fulfill, not abolish the law.[4] The law as conceived by the legalists of his day was to be fulfilled by carrying it up into a higher law of love and grace. These are the most profound aspects of both divine and human nature. Legalists have great difficulty in understanding them.

There is another implication in the attitude of Jesus. These legalistic people were really seeking something which they were not finding—freedom from anxiety and guilt. They were struggling with deep emotional and spiirtual problems and were suffering because they had not been able to find real answers. Their legalism was a distorted attempt at solution. It could not give them any real help. Jesus must have felt a deep compassion for them in their suffering— if he could only fulfill the need through love and grace which they were mistakenly trying to get fulfilled through legalism!

Jesus seems to have expressed this attitude to needy persons on several occasions. Two are recorded in the twelfth chapter of Matthew; the incident of his disciples gathering grain on the sabbath, and the healing of a man with a withered hand, both situations dealing with need, hunger and illness. In both cases he set aside legal requirements in favor of human values. Love and grace took precedence over compulsive adherence to rules. In this way Jesus dramatized his attitude, hoping perhaps to break through the rigid defenses the people had set up in order to protect themselves and their compulsions. But some of them were so fearful and anxious that they were inwardly forced to reject his appeal to love and grace, and therefore to reject him. In the same way such folk are today likely to reject help while they continue to hurt others by their sick attitudes. Emotional illness, especially when supported by religious sanctions, has a strong need to defend and propagate itself. This need may be mistaken for a genuine Christian motive.

Another way in which the Old Testament handled guilt feelings is illustrated in Psalm 51. Here we see a deep attitude of repentance, that is, a desire to change and get release from guilt feelings, along with an honest and humble confession which shares the feelings of guilt with God. The confessor relies on God's mercy, love and grace. Here is a high point of religious experience as it affects health. This kind of an experience leads to a release from guilt and a re-establishment of a relationship of devotion and love toward God. It is a profoundly therapeutic experience. It is the Old Testament's reach for the experience of forgiveness which is fully realized in the New Testament.

## Guilt and Forgiveness in the New Testament

Jesus was conscious of the reality of sin in human life, and understood its destructiveness. He did not try to explain it, but in the parable of the prodigal son,[5] and in his relationship with Zacchaeus,[6] Peter [7] and Judas,[8] to mention only a few, the emphasis is on redemption. But being conscious of the reality of sin did not mean that he was obsessed by the idea. His experience and his teaching was firmly rooted in a deeper Reality, the love and mercy of God. He saw beneath sin into deeper resources that made it possible to overcome sin. But this victory is not just a refusal to commit a specific act; it is an experience of loving fellowship with God and man which enabled him to become a creative, redemptive person rather than an estranged, destructive person. In this relationship of complete self-giving to God and man he found the fulfillment of himself and his own life. This is the difference between the legalistic prohibition of sinful acts which robs life of its vitality while it seeks to make artificial saints, and the overcoming of the destructive force of sin through a fellowship with God which releases love and faith for redemptive activity toward men. The life of Jesus has its great significance in its revelation of man's profound possibilities in fellowship with God.

The parable of the prodigal son illustrates the insight of Jesus into the nature of sin as estrangement and isolation. This young man was unable to accept the relationship which his father offered him, so he lived out his feelings of hostility and separation by making a physical separation. It would be hard to find a more vivid picture of the feeling of isolation than a lone individual sitting among the swine, hungry and apparently uncared for.

With rare insight, Jesus' story does not surround the prodigal with a flood of anxious helpers, all telling him what to do or offering their own patent solution. The boy comes to himself through the utilization of his own potentialities and the constructive elements which his previous wholesome relations with others had built into his personality. In the last analysis, no one but ourselves can break down the barriers which we set up within ourselves, though at times, when we really want it, skillful help from another person may be a necessary assistance.

When this boy became aware of the real nature of his situation he saw that the answer lay in a new kind of relationship with his father. The change had to take place within himself before there could be any change on the level of action. In his isolation he sought dependency on and satisfaction through other means than personal relationships, primarily symbolized by his material inherit- ance, but he found that this did not provide the answers to his underlying needs. These needs are to be satisfied only through a deep sense of belonging. "Thou hast made us for thyself and our hearts are restless until they find their rest in Thee," is Augustine's profound insight.

Jesus himself did not attempt to handle the problem of sin by easy answers. He had insight into each person's responsibility to deal with the barrier within himself. In his genuine respect for persons he did not seek to take this responsibility from them nor to infringe upon it.

But he did see that if a person is to break down the inner barrier to a sense of belonging, he must have something to assist him in the process. No man can carry on this struggle successfully by him- self. He has to be sure that when he reaches out from behind his inner barriers there will be someone there to receive and accept him. Indeed, he has to be sure of this before he reaches out; he cannot reach out to nothingness, nor to an abstract idea, but only to a

person whose love and acceptance have already been offered. It was
this kind of a relationship which Jesus offered in his everyday con-
tacts. It was this relationship which he offered to Zacchaeus, to the
woman taken in adultery [9] and even to her accusers, to Peter, to
Judas and others. The prodigal knew that his father was reaching
out to him before he could decide to return home.

But Jesus did not offer this loving acceptance simply of and by
himself. He felt this to be God's attitude toward men, the kind of
relationship which God was trying to offer men. Therefore men
could reach out toward God. God was a Father who felt a strong
love for his children, who accepted, forgave and re-established a
sense of togetherness. This was Jesus' experience of God; it was an
experience which he mediated to others. His revelation of God to
men was not contained in an idea but in a life which offered to men
what he had first experienced. He accepted men as children of God,
loved by God and therefore to be loved by him. There are questions
which are still unanswered, and perhaps forever will be, as to what
Jesus really thought of himself. But there can be no question as to
the kind of relationships he offered others, and no question that he
felt this was the way God would have it. Freely he had received
from God, freely he gave out of that abundance. This openhearted,
openhanded spirit was in strong contrast to the rejecting, censorious
attitude expressed by many "righteous" persons.

We have moved from Jesus' understanding of sin to his attitude
toward the sinner. This is an important step. One can understand
sin as an evil that needs to be eradicated from human life without
feeling that one must also eradicate the sinner. Many religious
persons have not learned to distinguish between the sin and the
sinner, and their attitudes toward others is one of harsh condemnation which only makes the barriers of separation deeper and
stronger. Such persons are reacting to their own feelings of guilt,
of which they are probably unaware. They are condemning others
for what they cannot handle successfully in themselves. Often they
condemn in the name of religion, and even represent their attitude
to be that of God. Not having found release from their own guilt,
they feel a need for punishment which they redirect to others in

whom they see their own weaknesses. Jesus told a parable [10] dealing with a servant who begged and was granted forgiveness, but who in turn was unwilling to forgive a fellow servant. He also exhorted his followers: "Judge not, that you be not judged." [11] Such judgment is really condemning in others what we cannot admit in ourselves.

Jesus' attitude toward the sinner has often been characterized as compassion. He seems indeed to have had an unusual capacity to feel deeply with others, to sense their suffering and to enable them to share it with him. He had a remarkable sensitivity to human need. He had no need to hurt, only to heal. Such profound compassion is a fundamental quality of human personality, but its expression is frequently blocked by fear and guilt.

Jesus had faced, struggled with and emerged victorious over these inner forces which make for isolation, as is described in his temptation experiences. He had discovered that he could be hurt by others, but that he did not have to respond by hurting them. He could offer a relationship which might help them to respond with acceptance and love, rather than hostility. Because he did not fear being hurt he could be compassionate, understanding, accepting and self-giving. The Cross is the supreme demonstration of this redemptive attitude.

While Jesus' acceptance of the sinner was grounded in an understanding of the sinner as a child of God, he certainly hoped for a positive response from the individual. He dealt with Peter and Judas in a manner designed to make it possible for them to acknowledge their weakness and accept the redemptive relationship which he offered. The same attitude is clear in his parable of the prodigal. In his treatment of Zacchaeus we see it again with an effective result. He felt free to associate with publicans and sinners, much to the disgust of the "righteous." Here again he was reaching out, hoping for and certainly at times receiving, a positive response which led to a changed way of life. He seemed to divide people into two classes, not saints and sinners, but the wise and foolish.[12] The wise are those who respond in a positive manner and accept a fellowship which gives stability and security even in the midst of destructive external circumstances. The foolish are those who respond in a negative manner and who therefore have only fear and hostility as a basis for meeting destructive circumstances. The wise are those who are able to respond in love and faith and in so doing are able to take advantage of new opportunities for growth and joy; the foolish are those whose lamps have been emptied of the oil of love and faith and who are therefore unable to enter into new opportunities. Jesus had compassion on these blocked individuals. His attitude seems to be reflected in a modern physician who remarked, "I could cure this patient of his illness if he could only accept the fact that I am trying to help him."

In this connection the statement of Jesus in regard to the unpardonable sin [13] needs some thought. If one tries to think of some "sin," that is, of some action which cannot be forgiven, he is baffled. If one thinks of sin as a relationship of separation and isolation, he meets a similar problem, for separation and isolation can be broken through. But if he thinks of the lack of desire and ability to accept a restored relationship on the part of some individuals, he gets a clue to the meaning of these words of Jesus. Basic to the restoration of a broken relationship is the desire to have it restored and a willingness to fulfill the conditions necessary for restoration. Sometimes these conditions are difficult and painful, and a person may feel strong resistances within himself. He may then reject acceptance; refuse to admit his need for forgiveness; in short, not want to be forgiven. Because forgiveness is always a mutual relationship, he may be successful in blocking it. He cannot be forgiven if he will not accept forgiveness.

What does this refusal to accept a restored relationship have to do with the words of Jesus about blasphemy against the Holy Spirit as the unforgivable sin? We must return again to the idea of spirit as the basic core of personality. It is the whole out of which feelings, attitudes, thoughts, actions emerge. It grows out of the quality of the relationships which we are now about to create or accept with others. We know the spirit of a man by the kind of relationships which he forms with others. Since holy is related to the idea of wholeness, the Holy Spirit is to be understood as the life of God in the soul of man inspiring man toward wholeness and oneness. The

Holy Spirit is present when God's relationship of redemptive love becomes actual in a person's experience. This acceptance of God's love may come about through a relationship with another person, through which one becomes aware of a need to change or to grow. To sin against the Holy Spirit is to say, "I do not want to be cured; I do not want to be whole; I have no need of help; I do not want a restored relationship; I have no sins, I do not need forgiveness." Obviously such a person is not aware of his need, so not being willing or able to admit it to himself or to another, he feels self-righteous, arrogant and superior. He possesses, or is possessed by, a spiritual blindness that confuses truth with error, and the work of the Holy Spirit with evil or demonic activity. Such a person will continue to deteriorate, for no one stays the way he is; life is not static. There is growth or regression; a movement toward health or toward illness; a re-establishment of broken relationships or a further separation.

The person who blasphemes against the Holy Spirit usually does not realize what he is doing, since he is suffering from a tremendous amount of ego inflation rooted in a deep sense of unworthiness. On the other hand, occasionally a person freely confesses committing the unpardonable sin. Such a person feels very guilty and is very sick emotionally. The idea that one has committed the unpardonable sin is a symptom of illness, and it is not to be taken literally. The person desperately needs help, but helping him is difficult and should be undertaken only by a trained psychiatrist.

Jesus not only had the capacity to sense the depth and intensity of guilt and the consequent suffering; he also had the capacity to see the relationship between feelings of guilt and illness. In fact these two capacities are related; one who has the first will have the second. There is a profound and real spiritual communication between persons when one feels another's suffering in love.

Jesus' insight into the relation of feelings of guilt and illness is clearly illustrated by the incident of the healing of the paralytic in Mark 2:1–12. This is undoubtedly a telescoped account of what actually happened, but certain aspects stand out. One is Jesus' ability to speak to the deeper levels of the sick man's mind. The word he spoke was one of forgiveness. A person who is sick because of feelings of guilt usually does not know consciously that he feels guilty. But Jesus, sensitive to the deeper forces in this man's experience, sensed the problem. There was no condemnation; there was forgiveness. And the results were quickly evident. Physical functions which are disturbed because of emotional tension quickly return to normal if the disturbance has not been of sufficient duration to result in actual organic change. Jesus mediated a deep love and forgiveness; the paralytic felt, accepted and responded to the relationship which Jesus offered him.

Another aspect that stands out is the questioning of the scribes "in their hearts." Apparently they said nothing, but Jesus again sensed their feelings and spoke directly to them. In this conversation Jesus clearly expresses the belief that offering the man forgiveness of sins and telling him to rise and walk were just saying the same thing in different words. The doubters could not accept the insights of Jesus because they had never experienced forgiveness, and had never felt its power. They are good examples of persons who have repressed their guilt and then have built up strong legalistic and rationalistic religious defenses against it. They make life very difficult for others, even to the blocking of mercy from others.

The insights of Jesus are elaborated by modern medicine which knows scientifically that feelings of guilt do make people sick, and that persons find release from such feelings when in a relationship of love and acceptance with another they are able to talk about their feelings and relate them specifically to the experiences out of which they arose. Sometimes symptoms are relieved quickly; sometimes time is required to restore physical functioning; sometimes organic conditions have become so fixed that they cannot be restored to normal.

There is a tendency to believe that all illness and suffering is produced by guilt or sin. Jesus had to deal with this idea. While he knew that some illness was grounded in guilt that needed forgiveness, he did not hold that all illness was due to guilt, nor that one could reason from misfortune back to guilt. Sensing what was in the minds of those who reported the slaying of some Galileans by

Pilate, he asked, "Do you think that these Galileans were worse sinners than all the other Galileans, because they suffered thus? I tell you, No; but unless you repent you will all likewise perish." [14] He used the falling of the tower of Siloam [15] as another illustration of the same attitude. He saw persons standing in need of a restored relationship through repentance, but he did not understand God as one who arbitrarily visited punishment on certain persons because of their sins. He did not attempt to explain certain kinds of suffering; but neither did he use suffering to inspire an unwarranted fear of God. He appealed to men on the basis of their need and their high possibilities; not on their fear of being struck dead or of getting ulcers.

Jesus faced the same problem when they brought a man blind from birth, asking, "Who sinned, this man or his parents, that he was born blind?" [16] He clearly rejected the idea that the man's blindness was proof of sin, and pointed out that suffering of this kind can be turned toward a redemptive purpose, for through it the work of God can be made manifest.

The explanation of this tendency to find sin as a cause for all suffering can only be found in the projection of our own feelings of guilt and our own need for punishment onto others. Feeling guilty, we also tend to feel hostile, and make others bear the brunt of our hostility on the ground that they are evil. With this shifting of responsibility comes a false feeling of self-righteousness. Thoroughly benevolent persons, such as Jesus, have no need to feel hostile to others, since they are free of such guilt and its resulting hostility and are able to give love and understanding. Thus our theological interpretations are frequently a reflection of our own inner condition.

Jesus had some other insights into forgiveness which are important from the point of view of health. He stresses forgiveness, not so much as an act, but as an attitude, a relationship. In response to Peter's question as to how often one should forgive a brother he said, "I do not say to you seven times, but seventy times seven." [17] Obviously this does not mean a mechanically calculated limit on forgiveness, but offering as much forgiveness as the offender requires.

Forgiveness is an attitude of acceptance; it is reacting to harm, not with hostility which hurts both parties, but with love which affirms the best in both persons. The person who says, "I will forgive but I will not forget," is continuing to hold his hostility and will suffer from it. The only way to prevent ourselves from being harmed emotionally and spiritually is by the kind of love which accepts those who hurt us while we try to bring reconciliation into the situation. Reconciliation requires a full facing of all of the realities, and this may be very painful and difficult. It is on this rock that much attempted forgiveness fails. Either forgiving or accepting forgiveness may require profound changes which one may not be ready or willing to make. The Christian relationship of forgiveness is not an easy, soft matter. It represents the achievement of a high level of spiritual maturity and the sacrifice of all of the inner attitudes and feelings that create barriers toward others.

Another insight in Jesus' teaching is important, namely, that we can be forgiven only as we forgive.[18] There is a fundamental psychological law here. Another way of expressing it is that we cannot accept forgiveness until we are also ready to give it, for really to accept mercy is to become merciful; to become merciful is to receive mercy. To accept forgiveness we must deal adequately with the inner attitudes and relationships out of which the guilt feeling arises. We cannot accept forgiveness for a feeling of hatred while we still hold on to the hatred. But it should be emphasized that we do not automatically or by some act of will "give up" such feelings; we may feel consciously that we have either forgiven or have been forgiven, when down in the deeper levels of our mind neither has taken place. Out of such tragic self-deception much illness arises. This is the insight in the parable of the servant [18] who would not forgive his debtors even though he expected to receive forgiveness from his master.

Turning to the meaning of the Christian idea of victory over sin, we find Paul interpreting this experience in terms of reconciliation. "God was in Christ reconciling the world to himself." [19] This would mean the overcoming of a sense of separation and the establishment of a sense of fellowship and belonging. It would also mean a sense of acceptance from God that would give a person sufficient strength to deal constructively with his feelings of guilt and with the situations out of which feelings of guilt arose. Forgiveness is not a matter of being excused from some wrongdoing. It is an experience of acceptance through which we become aware of inner resources which make it possible for us in turn to accept the responsibility of dealing with the roots of our wrongdoing. It is the expression of a kind of love which enables us to see what we may become; the kind of acceptance one should find in the Christian Church.

We need to understand this phrase of Paul's, "God was in Christ reconciling the world unto himself," as a theological interpretation of a religious experience in which a sense of God's acceptance becomes real emotionally. This is not an experience to be proved intellectually. An individual understands as a child understands that his mother loves him. The fact that frequently love gets mixed with anxiety and resentment may make it impossible, or very difficult, to feel this acceptance in relation to God.

Two other expressions of Paul's emphasize again the profound nature of Christian experience. "While we were yet sinners Christ died for us," [20] and, "Where sin increased, grace abounded all the more." [21]

In the first of these statements, we see clearly the experience of being loved and accepted even when we are most unlovable and unacceptable. In the second, we become aware of the fact that this love and acceptance is nothing which we can achieve through works. It is rather the gift of grace, that is, it is freely given out of God's love for us. Furthermore, grace is deeper and more powerful than sin. When they are properly appropriated the redemptive or curative forces are stronger than the forces that make for sin and illness. Much of the tension of human life comes from a feeling of being rejected or unacceptable and much of the strength of human life comes from knowing that we are accepted, even though we feel unworthy of that acceptance. In a relationship of acceptance we have a basis for growing into a full measure of self-acceptance and self-responsibility. The love and acceptance of God can be communicated to us on the level of ideas such as are presented by Paul, but if this communication remains on an intellectual level, it may not bring release. The kind of communication that releases a sense of unworthiness and guilt is that in which we experience the reality of love and forgiveness in an actual relationship. This is the kind of communication that men have felt in their experience of Christ.

The struggle to accept the acceptance of Christ is illustrated by the experience of Judas [8] and Peter.[7] From our records there is evidence that Christ attempted to establish with each of them the same kind of relationship. Peter found it difficult for a while to accept Christ's acceptance of him, which is expressed in the words of Christ, "I have prayed for you that your faith may not fail; and when you have turned again, strengthen your brethren." Indeed Peter had to go through the process of rejecting Christ before finally he could come to an experience of accepting fully Christ's acceptance. This meant a radical change in his attitudes and goals. Judas, on the other hand, faced a similar problem but he did not work through his attitudes to the point where acceptance of Christ's acceptance was possible. He was one of the unfortunate humans whose personality was so deeply distorted that he had to respond with hostility rather than love to Christ.

Any pastor who has done much counseling understands what we are facing here. There are many people who find it difficult to look at themselves in conversation with another person because of the difficulty of trusting the other person deeply enough. Even in consulting a pastor, people require varying periods of time to come into a deep enough trust to share some life burden with him. At first they cannot accept the pastor's acceptance of them as real and trustworthy, but through a series of conversations in which their problem is explored, they come to feel understood, and therefore able to respond with trust. But some are completely unable to accept love and understanding.

In addition to the influence of previous experience on our ability to accept love, there is also the capacity to become aware of and to evaluate our own reactions, and to decide whether our pattern of reaction can be continued with satisfaction. For instance, we may want to get well or we may want to remain sick. We may want to solve our problems or we may want to continue in our problems. We may want to accept love or we may want to hold on to our hostilities. The capacity to evaluate and to determine what our responses shall be becomes weakened through emotional conflict or strengthened through experiences in which we come to understand ourselves in a relationship of trust with another person.

There is a certain element of judgment in the experience of being accepted. It is not a judgment which another renders on us through condemnation, but a self-judgment which we feel because of our relationship with a stronger, more mature or more loving person. This kind of self-judgment is essential for growth. Condemnation by another puts us on the defensive, and makes growth difficult or impossible; genuine love and acceptance by one stronger than ourselves leads to self-judgment, and at times to a radical crisis. But to be accepted by a person who confirms the weakness, evil or neurosis in us is to be encouraged to remain in that condition. The difference between these attitudes should be the difference between the acceptance we find in the Church and the acceptance we find in a liquor tavern.

This need for love and acceptance has a profound significance for the work of the Church, for the Church must not only interpret the Christian Gospel in terms of ideas, but its more significant task is to mediate to men the experience of God's acceptance and love. The Christian Church has had certain practices designed to help individuals to grow into an acceptance of the Gospel. One of these is confession.[22] This practice is deeply rooted in the Christian faith, but in many of our Protestant churches we have seriously neglected it. It is not the confession in the formal, ritualistic sense which needs restoration, but confession in a genuine and realistic sense. The modern movement known as pastoral counseling is bringing us back to a greater appreciation of the need which each of us has at certain times for the unburdening of ourselves and for the sharing of our painful experiences with another person who represents what to us is ultimate in life.

Confession is a revealing of ourselves to God and to ourselves through communication with a pastor who both represents God to us and us to God. It involves a profound sense of honesty, a discovery of that in ourselves which really needs to be confessed, a distinguishing between that which is imaginary evil and that which is real evil, a sorting out and honest facing of our basic attitudes toward ourselves and toward others and toward God. It involves a relating of actual feelings of guilt to the experiences out of which the guilt arose, and a relinquishing of the feeling of guilt when the necessary growth has been achieved.

Handling confessions or pastoral counseling requires a kind of training for the pastor which the Church is not now affording him in sufficient measure. It also involves a rather radical revision of the work of the pastor so that time is available for individuals who need to share some burden with him. We are doing people an injustice if on Sunday we help them to discover areas in their life which need correction and revision, but during the week no one with adequate training is available to give them the specific help which they need.

With confession the Christian faith has always coupled repentance.[23] Repentance is not a feeling of self-punishment, but rather the experience of being willing and able to make a change in our feelings and attitudes. It is a change in which we take an active part; not something which is done to us. We repent; God does not repent for us. Sometimes we find it easy to believe that God must make the necessary changes in us. At such times, we do not want to take the responsibility of facing, understanding, and making desirable changes in attitudes and relationships. Repentance is not an act of will, but an experience of growth in which harmful attitudes and desires are renounced, and mature, Christian attitudes are accepted as valid and determining for oneself. This experience of growth may take a shorter or longer period of time, depending on the person. But it cannot take place except through a living relationship with a person or group in which redemptive love is accepted. Repentance is the gateway to a fuller life. It is a constant experience for those who maintain a living relationship with Christ, as in this relationship there is a continuous awareness of areas in which growth or change is needed.

*Chapter Four*

# Love, Hate and Health

EVERY Christian is familiar with the great commandment of Jesus that we should love God with our whole being and our neighbor as ourselves.[1] In a much later day, Sigmund Freud, the founder of psychoanalysis, gave a judgment from a different point of view: "In the last resort we must begin to love in order that we may not fall ill, and must fall ill, if in consequence of frustration, we cannot love." [2] And even more recently another psychoanalyst, Eric Fromm, has written, "Analytic therapy is essentially an attempt to help the patient gain or regain his capacity for love." [3] Not only for religion, but for health, love seems to be of central importance.

Men become ill if they cannot fulfill the conditions necessary to health, and health means wholeness. Love cannot be thought of as a part of the organism, as we might think of the stomach; it is rather a quality of relationship within oneself and between oneself and others, which influences the functioning of the organism toward wholeness. Love binds together, while its absence creates conflict, disintegration and illness. Love always seeks a closeness, a warmth, a union of one kind or another with a loved object. The nature and form of this relationship may vary from stage to stage in childhood and maturity, but in essence it always affirms the worth of the other as a person. It is in itself an expression of the need for wholeness in human relationships; only in loving relationships do we become our true selves.

If love is so fundamental both to religion and health, why is it that we have so many problems with love and why is it that we cannot love as we should? Why are we so defensive when told that we should love? We have a profound need for love, but we often call it impractical, visionary, idealistic and not of this world. Yet we cannot escape from it, nor stop talking and singing about it. Sometimes we reject it when we need it most; we cannot accept it, yet we demand it. We say it is unreal while we know it is the most real thing in life. We want to love yet we feel guilty and inhibited when we try to express love. Why is love so much of a problem? Perhaps in studying the relation of love to illness and health we find some insights into these questions.

Guilt and anxiety, as we have seen, are two obstacles to love; so are hate or hostility. When we feel guilty or anxious about any kind of love, hate or hostility in some form is also present. When we do not feel we are loved, or when we feel unable to love, these negative, destructive feelings are present, even though we may not consciously recognize them.

Remembering the experience of John, the man who was afraid something would happen to his wife, we recall that the source of his fear was his strong resentment toward her, which he pushed to the back of his mind. Later, he was not aware of his resentment; only of his fear. In our culture people have many resentments and hatreds, some hidden and some open. This is not a new situation in the history of mankind; there are passages in the Bible which record the anger and hatred of men in centuries long past.

The ability to be angry is deeply rooted in human nature. A very small infant can become angry to the point of rage. For the infant, as for all of us, anger is a response made to an experience of frustration which makes us fearful and insecure. It calls attention to the fact that something is wrong in our relationships, usually to the fact that we do not feel loved. On the other hand, since its aim is either to destroy the offender, or get away from him, there are many human situations where anger only creates greater danger. The small child, for example, may get very angry at a parent and feel a wish to destroy the parent; but the small child also needs the parent, and to destroy or withdraw from him is only to put himself in a worse situation. This is true of many human relationships. To express anger openly often creates more frustration, fear and insecurity. It is part of the process of growing from infancy to maturity to learn when and what are appropriate expressions of anger.

When a child becomes afraid of his own anger, he has to bury it, and hide it deeply inside himself. Anger thus held in festers and becomes a poison. It then begins to emerge in disguised ways, such as unruly behavior or physical sickness. It is this bottled-up, festering anger which we term resentment, hostility or hatred; all feelings which make us want to hurt someone, and the ultimate expression of hurting is killing.

We cannot understand anger and hatred without understanding their relationship to love, for the primary and most profound frustration out of which anger grows is the frustration of love. The deepest need that any human being has is the need for closeness with other significant persons. We all need to be at one with certain others. This is what love means in its most profound sense; a relationship in which we feel at one, united, belonging, accepted, respected. For the child to be punished when he expresses anger, or for him to live continually, or even intermittently, in an atmosphere where he is not loved, is to place him in a situation where his anger turns to hostility. This fact means that every child will have some anger and will have some resentment and hostility toward his parents, for no parents, being human, are capable of constantly and consistently giving their child perfect love. This fact has deep significance for us and for religion.

There is no question about the place of hostility in the creation of illness. When combined with anxiety, guilt and shame, as it usually is, hostilities present a condition in which the human body and mind function only with difficulty, or drive the person almost beyond the limits of his strength. Thus these tensions, in various combinations, are present in much physical illness, through their power to inhibit or overstimulate organic functioning. Here the hostility is unconsciously expressed through some organ of the body, or finds expression through other distorted forms of behavior, or irrational ideas. Much of the rebellious behavior of children is rooted in hostility, and such feelings play a large part in juvenile delinquency, which is in itself an illness. In many of the forms of illnesses called neuroses or psychoses, hostilities seem to be turned against oneself so that one's own personality is injured. Hostilities also play a large part in certain accidents, a person wanting to injure himself or another. Many make themselves fail in some desirable enterprise due to an unconscious need to hurt themselves. Hostilities are also the root of many marriage problems. In marriage a husband works out against his wife hostilities which developed originally against his mother or some other adult in his childhood. Likewise, unhealthy hostilities often find expression in religious activities and behavior, such as condemning those who do not share our beliefs.

Just as anger and related feelings are causative factors in much illness, so love is fundamental in the prevention and cure of illness. Love recognizes the other person as unique and distinct, much like yet different from oneself, and so due the respect which one desires for himself. Love recognizes the other as a person whose needs we may help to meet, but whose destiny we have no right to control, whose privacy we have no right to invade, whose life we have no right to exploit for our own ends. Love recognizes that what we do for another must be governed by what the other needs and is willing to accept from us. These relationships have different meanings on different age levels.

To the small infant, love is largely a matter of receiving from the mother or other adults. The infant's needs are great, his dependency is great, he must be given to by persons who are warm, accepting, gentle, understanding, and who do not resent having the responsibility for him nor having to give to him. For the small infant, love and food become synonymous experiences; he takes in love with his food if the mother's attitude is one of warm, generous concern for him. Such love bridges the gap between the mother and child as separate, distinct organisms or persons and gives the child a sense of belonging with the mother because that is the way the mother feels and responds to the child. Even in an atmosphere of this kind there will be inevitable frustrations, and in such times the child will feel anger, but because of the deeper sense of security he will gradually learn how to handle this anger. Unless they are oversevere, he will learn how to deal with inevitable frustrations. If, however, the child feels rejection and resentment on the part of the mother in his feeding-handling-bathing relationships he will not feel that he really belongs, will find it hard to receive from his mother, and will become anxious and hostile.

Love is often interpreted to mean that there shall be no limit placed on the activities of the child, and no punishment of any kind. But when this concept of love is examined in the light of the needs of the child, it is seen to be faulty because one of his needs is for a clearly structured, well-ordered world in which he can feel secure. Too much permissiveness may make him feel as anxious as too much restriction. Since he has very few, if any, inborn patterns of behavior, and since he must learn most of his patterns, he is dependent on his environment to indicate to him what patterns are acceptable. He needs to know what is involved in his relationships with other persons, and what is expected of him in the community of which he is a part. If more is expected than he can give, or if expectations are enforced with severity, he will feel an unnecessary burden of anxiety and hostility.

On the other hand, unrestricted freedom gives the child a completely false conception of himself in relationship with others. It results in an artificially inflated ego; he grows up making impossible demands on others and refusing to accept any of the demands that life makes on him. He becomes the law for himself and those about him, rather than accepting law that is inherent in life. Unrestricted freedom creates an overevaluation of the self much the same as occurs in the child who is dominated and who responds in rebellion against that domination.

Genuine love means helping the child to accept those conditions which life imposes on all of us and those laws which are essential for satisfying group relationships. Thus the parent must be an authority to the child and at the same time give the child freedom to grow. Neither the freedom nor the authority should be arbitrary; the child should be helped to see that there are genuine reasons for

the restrictions and that his freedom is also genuine. To tell a child
that he may make up his own mind as long as he makes it up our
way is hardly genuine freedom and will be felt by the child as
unjust.

A genuine attitude of love will accept the child's natural feelings
of rebellion and help him to deal with them. A genuine love will also
learn from the child. The parent will be quick to sense that the
child's anxiety or rebellion is an indication that the parent has imposed restrictions too severely, or that the child needs help in understanding, or that something else is wrong in the parent's relationship
to the child. No parent can be perfect; but one of the ways he can
improve is by allowing the child to teach him as he seeks to teach
the child.

What this all means in terms of specific situations depends on
the age of the child. About the age of two the child will commence
to show rebellion against too many restrictions and indicate that he
wants to make up his own mind in some things. At this age the
need for autonomy emerges strongly in the child, although it is
balanced by a need for dependency and support. Sometimes the
need for autonomy emerges in negative terms and the child learns
to say "No" with emphasis. This makes some parents anxious and
they react with more firmness and even severity. The child is really
trying to learn in small ways to be autonomous just as he had to
learn to walk by taking tiny steps. In his desire to be autonomous
he still needs to hold on to someone, and he will continue to do this
for a long time if the relationship is one which gives direction and
support while allowing freedom where he is able to use it. This is
one of the meanings of love at this age; a relationship of warmth,
understanding and acceptance which gives both direction and freedom so that the child in turn feels security and a sense of belonging
with the parent. The child is a separate person, and has to learn to
become more and more of a person in his own right; but he still
needs a large measure of direction and support in order to feel that
he belongs to others.

The child from three to six wants and needs a little more freedom
in some things, but he still wants and needs the support and direc-

tion of his parents. Changes taking place within him which are part of his natural growth require some new concrete expressions of love. He is becoming aware of himself as a member of one of the sexes and he is commencing to discover the difference between the sexes. He is asking questions about where babies come from or where he came from. The boy may be more closely attached to his mother and the girl to her father, and each may show some antagonism to the parent of the same sex. At this stage the child is learning something new to him about what it means to be a man and a woman and how men and women relate to each other. Of course his learning is not intellectual; it is emotional learning and it is achieved as he feels the relation of the parents to each other and to him. The questions of the child about sex should be answered with both adequate facts and emotional understanding; answering these questions in a mood of anxiety or guilt about sex may create similar feelings in the child. The child's attachment to the parent of the opposite sex should be accepted and understood as a normal phase of life, neither to be condemned nor overencouraged. Love at this age means giving the child understanding, acceptance and direction in a manner which continues his sense of security with and belonging to his parents as a growing person. This kind of support will give him a basis for learning to use himself and his body creatively, and for developing a wholesome relationship with his own and the opposite sex in adolescence and in adult life.

As the child moves into adolescence he has much the same needs, but in a different balance. He still needs the support and understanding of his parents, he needs some direction and authority but also greater freedom. If a sharing and acceptance of his feelings has been experienced in childhood, he will now continue to share his experiences and feelings, not so much for the purposes of receiving authoritative answers as for working through to his solutions of his own problems. Adolescence is the bridge between childhood and maturity and in this period much of the dependence on parents must be left behind if the child is to grow toward autonomous, responsible maturity. Parental love for the adolescent means in part the parent's willingness to give him up, but as has been frequently pointed out, it is less painful for many mothers to give birth to the child than to loose the emotional cords of control and authority in the adolescent period. Fathers may have the same problem. Anxiety and guilt in parents about their own adolescence make them fearful for the child, and in their fear they hold on. This either brings a reaction of submissiveness or rebellion in the child, and while rebellion is preferable to submissiveness from the point of view of health, either may lead to unhappy adulthood. The goal of adolescence is the emergence of an adult who is an autonomous, responsible person capable of a mature love for his parents and for others. Through such love and respect he continues to experience for himself, and to give to others, a sense of security and belonging, while also achieving the uniqueness of his own individuality.

In infancy, love is largely an experience of receiving. The infant has little to give, but he learns to give in small ways as he receives. His ability to give grows through each stage of life until in maturity he has learned to give in a more complete manner. While things have an importance in every phase of life, his growth requires that his parents give of themselves. Many parents who do not love their child in a genuine manner try to make it up to them by giving things, only to find that the child is rudely ungrateful. The child resents that he does not have the genuine concern of his parents, and finds it hard to learn to love in the sense of giving himself. This capacity to give oneself is one of the characteristics of mature love. It is essential to any close relationship, and is certainly one of the goals of the Christian faith.

A spontaneous quality distinguishes the genuine giving of oneself from legalistic forms of behavior which often pass for love. Love of this kind cannot be forced by conscience nor by will power. On the other hand, its spontaneous expression can be inhibited by a sense of guilt or anxiety. We cannot give unless we have first been given to; we learn to love by being loved. There is no escaping the complete mutuality and interdependence which we humans have with one another.

Maturity means the capacity to give love in terms of giving oneself, even though at times one does not receive love. To love those who love us is not so difficult; children can do this. But to love those who do not love us or those who seem to us to be very unlovable, this is more difficult and requires more maturity. Part of a mature person's sense of belonging to a group is not only that he is loved and accepted by the group, but that he has the inner strength to give love even under adverse conditions. Much of our need for belonging is satisfied only as we feel able to give something of value to the group. It is characteristic of many forms of sickness that the person cannot give. We find fulfillment of ourselves and the full significance of membership in a group only as we are able to give as well as to receive.

It is thus no accident that more than one writer in the field of psychotherapy, the art of treating emotional illnesses, stresses the idea that his task is to teach his patient how to love. He does this teaching by allowing and encouraging the patient to unburden his anxieties, guilts and hostilities in a relationship of understanding and acceptance. In this way the patient comes to experience the love of the therapist, an attitude which seeks to help the patient discover and become himself, and the patient learns to replace the feelings that tend to create illness with love and faith. The sick person often finds it necessary to learn to see and accept the love that is all about him but which he has not been able to accept because of his anxieties.

## Anger and Hatred in the Bible

One of the early studies of anger in the Bible is the story of Cain and Abel,[4] a story that has been repeated many times. Modern psychologists have a term for it, "sibling rivalry," by which they mean the rivalry of children for the love and approval of the parents. In this story Abel's offering was accepted and he therefore felt accepted. Cain's was not, and he felt rejected. The little offerings a child brings to parents are very important, as they represent the child, and the acceptance or rejection of the child. Cain's hostility and jealousy became a barrier separating him from his brother. The separation was completed in the slaying of Abel. Cain is an example of an immature person whose hostilities lead him to compete with another person rather than to make his own achievement for the sake of the achievement itself. A more mature person would have rejoiced in his brother's success, and would have set about to improve his own work, not in competition with his brother, but for the sake of the work itself.

We see a reaction similar to Cain's in Jesus' story of the prodigal son,[5] where the elder brother, apparently too anxious and dependent to leave home, became angry and jealous at the reception his wayward brother received upon his return home. The elder brother was evidently glad that his younger brother had gone and did not want him to return. The parable does not give a final outcome, but suggests that the need for repentance on the part of the elder brother is just as real as the younger brother's need for repentance. Actually persons such as the younger brother may find it easier to deal with their problem than do persons such as the elder brother.

Another story repeated in many families is that of the rivalry of Joseph and his brothers.[6] The story is simple; Joseph, the son of his father's old age, becomes his father's favorite and brings the jealousy of his brothers upon his head. His favored position evidently makes him conceited, for he has dreams of his own greatness and does not see the impropriety of relating his dreams to his brothers. It is often true that in such situations the one who seems to be sinned against stimulates the aggressors in a subtle way, and then manages to place all of the blame on them. The brothers developed murderous impulses which would have been carried out were it not for one of them who evidently felt more love for the father and the brother than did the rest.

The insight throughout the Bible is that the ultimate end of anger and hatred is murder. The need to curb this danger rose out of human experience. "Thou shalt not kill"[7] became a commandment as men discovered that killing was contrary to the very nature of reality, the law of God and the welfare of the community. But men have learned that law alone is not sufficient to curb murder. The only answer is the development of persons whose capacity for love has grown to the extent that their love can master their hate.

√ But there is one expression of hatred, approved in the Old Testament, that is very significant for health. It is in the idea of hating evil. God is pictured as hating evil. "There are six things which the Lord hates," according to the writer of Proverbs.[8] The writer of the fifth Psalm sees God as hating all evildoers. God's hatred of evil was related to man's suffering as man interpreted his suffering as punishment for his evil-doing. "For we are consumed by thy anger; by thy wrath we are overwhelmed." [9] "There is no soundness in my flesh because of thy indignation; there is no health in my bones because of my sin." [10] Man has always had to account for the fact that there are painful, destructive elements in his experience, and he has interpreted these as expressing anger in God, through an analogy with human anger. What he saw in his own life revealed to him something of the nature of God.

Because God hated evil, so man should hate evil. Amos [11] puts it concisely, "hate evil, and love good." Micah [12] spoke of those who reversed this principle: "You who hate the good and love the evil." The writer of the ninety-seventh Psalm felt that "the Lord loves those who hate evil."

These insights may be related to an interpretation rather generally accepted in psychological circles today, that man has within himself this capacity for hatred, that this is an aspect of his experience which he cannot completely eradicate, that it has in it seeds of self-destruction in illness of one kind or another. But man can learn to redirect hatred so that its destructive force is spent against real evils rather than against persons. The Old Testament does not for a moment cover up the fact of man's hatred and destructiveness; it points man to the use of hate in the destruction of evil under the direction of love of the good.

## The Teaching of Jesus about Anger and Love

√ Any person who attempts to bring healing to man's body, mind or spirit must ultimately deal with the experience of anger and hatred. Jesus faced this necessity. He offered some profound insights into the nature of anger and love. He revealed a relationship of love toward God which he interpreted as grounded in God's love for him. He knew the profound destructiveness of hate and the strengthening, creative power of love.

We turn first to his teaching about anger and love as found in the Sermon on the Mount, in which he brings out what modern psychologists have also discovered, that it is not just behavior which is destructive, but even more destructive is the inner feeling of anger when held in and unresolved, and hence hardened into resentment, hostility and hatred.

Jesus [13] speaks of the danger of judgment which is the religious expression for what the psychologists mean by self-destructiveness. "You have heard that it was said to the men of old, 'You shall not kill; and whoever kills shall be liable to judgment.' But I say to you that everyone who is angry with his brother shall be liable to judgment; whoever insults his brother shall be liable to the council, and whoever says, 'You fool!' shall be liable to the hell of fire. So if you are offering your gift at the altar, and there remember that your brother has something against you, leave your gift there before the altar and go; first be reconciled to your brother, and then come and offer your gift. Make friends quickly with your accuser, while you are going with him to court, lest your accuser hand you over to the judge, and the judge to the guard, and you be put in prison; truly, I say to you, you will never get out till you have paid the last penny."

Anger, if intense or if allowed to become chronic, does burn us out, making love impossible and leaving a marked sense of insecurity and emptiness. It leads to illness in one form or another. Human relationships grounded in these feelings destroy; it is as if a man expects to nourish his body on poison. Jesus was a healer. He continues his discussion of anger in terms of the relationships involved and introduces together two ideas: worship and reconciliation. Anger separates man from man and creates a sense of insecurity; love moves to bring persons together; it reconciles. And so Jesus points out the necessity of taking the initiative in becoming reconciled with those who are angry at us.

Anger aims at the destruction of its object, usually another person.

It arises when we are denied something we want, but since it aims at destruction of another it also prevents us from receiving what we most need, love. It is therefore self-destructive. In suggesting an attitude of reconciliation Jesus seems to be hoping that his followers will develop sufficient inner strength and maturity that they will respond to his hunger with the reassurance of love which removes the need to be angry. Now this can be done only by the person who has mastered his own angers and fears so that they do not control his reactions. To follow this teaching requires a level of maturity which is the opposite of the neurotic attitudes suffered by many today. It also means that one needs to be free of anger and hostility of which he is not aware.

To respond to an angry man on a level deeper than his anger, that is, on the level of his hunger for love, is to offer reconciliation. It is to resolve the conflict and achieve a mutual sense of belonging. The entire Christian fellowship is at stake here. Many in our churches have not learned this way of reconciliation. For people to become angry within the Church is inevitable; for them to protect their anger and allow it to become divisive is both neurotic and non-Christian. To use their anger as a starting place for understanding one another and seeking fulfillment rather than destruction is to follow in the way of Christ. Our own need to be angry is curiously diminished as we seek the fulfillment of the legitimate needs of others. For in the very love we are able to give others we find a reassurance against the destructiveness which we feel unconsciously within ourselves.

Why is anger related to reconciliation and worship? Here is Jesus' insight that relationships on the human level foster or block relationships between man and God. For the goal of worship is to break through the sense of separation and become reconciled to God. To seek this reconciliation with God while we are not reconciled with man is to create a division within our lives. It forces us to push back our angers and hostilities, pretending that we do not have them or that they are justified, ignoring or repressing the guilt which we feel about our relationships. This is the reason why so much of our worship is actually unhealthy; we attempt to do the very thing which Jesus indicates is a harmful procedure. Many times our churches foster this unhealthy worship; we are often urged to come to worship, but are we ever helped to find reconciliation with others before coming? What would happen if, after a call to worship at eleven o'clock on Sunday morning, each of us who felt that our brother has something against us would quickly file out of our pews. It would upset the service, but religion would become dynamic and creative! But creative religion would upset the accepted order much further, so we conform to custom and become unhealthy. Persons who have been helped with hostilities through pastoral counseling often return to tell the pastor that they have suddenly and spontaneously found a new meaning and freedom in worship.

Jesus next shifts his figure of speech, but not his idea. We are to make friends with our accuser while we are going with him to court, lest something serious happen to us. Here is another insight which is confirmed in modern psychology. We cannot temporize with anger and hatred without intensifying or crystallizing it; we cannot see just how far we can go without disastrous consequences; we cannot continue to defend and justify our anger without its taking over and mastering us. Jesus gives us a word picture of the court and the judge to express what the psychologist says when he tells us that the inner structure of personality becomes hardened and sick through holding on to and fostering hostile, destructive feelings. The day may come when this process cannot be reversed; we are literally imprisoned by our own hostilities. And there are no five easy steps which will help us to freedom!

Jesus [14] further elaborates his insight in another figure of speech. He contrasts the "eye-for-an-eye" method of handling hurts with a turn-the-other-cheek approach. This advice has puzzled many people. It has been called impossible, impractical, and so it is for many people. We must remember that Jesus is describing attitudes which are achieved only through a high level of emotional and spiritual maturity. They cannot be practiced by immature persons, nor by persons with neurotic patterns of relationships. The neurotic person responds to being hurt either with hostility or with a kind of submissiveness which perverts the meaning of Jesus' words. Jesus is pointing to a level of maturity which seeks the fulfillment of the wrongdoer. To turn the other cheek is to take the initiative in seeking to form this relationship. It is to turn love toward those who hurt us. To be sure we may get hurt. Getting hurt may be necessary to another's redemption. Jesus got hurt, but he accepted the suffering in order to indicate that there is such a thing as a love that can be hurt without hurting back. It is possible to achieve this level of being. Persons can grow to the place where they can go far beyond the demands that others make on them in a way that seeks to redeem the aggressor. The center of Jesus' thought is always the kind of relationships which make growth, fulfillment and redemption possible. He understood that the response made by the person receiving the hurt was crucial. He was, and he tried to help others become, the kind of person who could overcome his own destructiveness and develop redeeming relationships with others.

Jesus [15] carries his teaching through to the relationship with one's enemies; this too is to be one of love. Modern man has a hard time with this attitude. But seen from the point of view of what love does to those who give it and receive it, and likewise what hate does to each, it makes sense. To say that another does not deserve to have love is also saying that I do not deserve to have it. To say that my hatred for him is justified is to say that his hatred for me is justified. Constantly Jesus held all men in equal relationship to one another as sons of a Creator-Father who loves them equally, in spite of the fact that they are at times unlovable. In Jesus' view we are to love because we find our deepest fulfillment in love, especially in loving the unlovable. No one is so unlovable as the one who wants to hurt us. Our impulse is to hit back. As children we love because we are loved. As mature Christians we are to love even those who would hurt us, as this is the only way to their redemption and to ours. Our own redemption, and also our health, is grounded in a relationship that is also redemptive for those who would hurt us. This is what perfection in love means; learning to use our redemptive potentiality to the fullest.

One of the curious aspects of human nature that many religious leaders have commented on is our capacity to hate that which is good. Jesus [16] spoke of this proclivity on a number of occasions. Men hate the righteous; evil men hate the light of truth because it exposes their evil; Christians should expect the world to hate them. The elder brother was angry at his father's goodness.

An outstanding illustration of this tendency to hate the good is to be found in the persecution conducted against the early Christians by Saul of Tarsus.[17] Saul felt the spontaneous love of the Christians as a threat to the kind of attitudes and relationships which he had developed on the basis of a strict legalism, and responded defensively by seeking to destroy the Christians. Like people who act under unconscious drives toward destructiveness, he did not understand his own actions, but "What I hate, that I do." [18] Through his relationship with Christians who could continue to love in spite of his destructiveness, the conflict surged to a climax in which the creative, loving aspects of his personality become dominant over the destructive. This conflict and its solution was expressed in the Epistle to the Galatians. Through Christ he had found release from his destructiveness into a new life of goodness and joy. He no longer needed to hate the good, as he no longer needed to fear it. The meaning of Christ is distorted by persons with such intense negative feelings and hence their need for a long relationship with others who can mediate to them something of the genuine love which is in Christ.

Jesus [19] again shows his insight into the dynamics of human personality in his sayings about love, forgiveness and judgment. "Judge not, and you will not be judged; condemn not, and you will not be condemned; forgive, and you will be forgiven; give, and it will be given to you; good measure, pressed down, shaken together, running over, will be put into your lap. For the measure you give will be the measure you get back." The judgment of which Jesus speaks here is a hostile judgment, the kind that is grounded in our own unreleased guilt. We project this guilt and the weakness out of which it grows on others and then attack them. This guilt and its resulting hostility blocks love and forgiveness. Forgiveness is the full acceptance of a person as a person in spite of his weaknesses. It costs something to forgive; we must give up those attitudes which separate us from

others and make us want to hurt them. It costs something to forgive; we must give up those attitudes which separate us from others
and make us want to hurt them. It costs something to be forgiven;
we must give up the pride which leads to self-defense, and accept
our tendency to hurt others as a part of ourselves which needs to be
changed. Forgiveness, given and received, is an essential experience
in becoming our real selves, as that in us which leads us not to
forgive nor to accept forgiveness is not our real self, but a well-
defended weakness in ourselves.

The experience of accepting forgiveness breaks through the barriers of guilt and hostility and frees us to give ourselves. This giving
we recognize as our real self. We want to do it. There is no sense
of ought nor compulsion, but a spontaneous being of oneself. This
is illustrated in the encounter of Jesus with the sinful woman,[20]
her subsequent anointing of his feet as a symbolic act of love, and
his comments to Simon's criticism of her act. Jesus' insight here—
"her sins, which are many, are forgiven, for she loved much; but he
who is forgiven little, loves little"—describes what happens to some
people who are forced by the very weight of their guilt to seek help.
They emerge with a capacity for love more developed than many
who have not been forced to a deep examination and modification
of their inner feelings and attitudes.

When we feel separated and guilty we do many things which are
labeled "sins," which are really attempts to call attention to our
inner plight and at the same time to justify it. Forgiveness is the act
of love in reaching across the barrier of separation, the "dividing
wall of hostility" as Paul [21] puts it, to give acceptance to a person in
spite of his feelings of unworthiness. It is looking beneath the
unworthiness to the real person to find there one who is worthy of
acceptance. It is the re-establishment of a feeling of belonging
through which anxiety is gradually released and growth takes place.
There are times when this must involve a long process of painfully
working through patterns of negative feeling and behavior that are
hardened. To attempt an easy, quick or forced change at such times
is likely to be disastrous.

How does man find the strength to love? The teachings of Jesus are clear on this; by realizing within himself that he is loved. God's love for man is a central theme in the teachings of Jesus from which man's love for his fellow men cannot be divorced.

Jesus felt and thought and spoke of God in terms of a loving father. The word "father" expressed a depth and a breadth of meaning that he had realized in his own experience. Various words involving relationships such as "father" take on a meaning that expresses our actual experience. To many persons today this word brings up negative feelings—anxiety, rebellion, resentment, guilt. But to Jesus its connotations were positive; God was love in the sense of creating men as his sons; in the sense of endowing them with potentialities like unto himself and then permitting them the freedom to find the fulfillment of these potentials; in the sense of recognizing them as persons with whom he desires fellowship and makes fellowship possible; sons in the sense of being separate, self-determining beings, with a responsibility for themselves, yet also a creative relationship to him. "Father" was a symbol which to Jesus was both adequate—as adequate as any form can be—and also authentic in its portrayal of the nature of God in his own experience.

At the very beginning of his ministry, at his baptism, he felt this relationship, "Thou art my beloved Son; with thee I am well pleased." [22] A similar realization was part of the experience of the transfiguration, "This is my beloved Son, with whom I am well pleased; listen to him." [23] When Jesus taught his disciples to pray he began, "Father, hallowed be thy name." [24] When he indicated the relationship of a believer to himself and to God, he said, "So every one who acknowledges me before men, I also will acknowledge before my Father who is in heaven." [25] In his picture of the last judgment, when men were judged in relation to their own love and mercy to other men, the King said, "Come, O blessed of my Father." [26] In a passage in which he expressed his awareness of the conflict between himself and the Pharisees and his compassion for the heavy laden, Jesus said, "I thank thee, Father, Lord of heaven and earth, that thou hast hidden these things from the wise and understanding and revealed them to babes; . . . All things have been delivered to me by my Father. . . . Come to me. . . ." [27] And as Jesus faced his most crucial moments, in Gethsemane and on the Cross, his prayers expressed an intimacy of relationship out of which deep strength was derived. "Abba, Father, all things are possible to thee; remove this cup from me; yet not what I will, but what thou wilt." [28] "Father, forgive them; for they know not what they do." [29] "Father, into thy hands I commit my spirit!" [30] In the Gospel of John there are also many passages where this relationship is expressed in a very vivid manner.

Jesus portrayed the love of God in his relationships to persons. Almost any page of the Gospels provides an illustration of this [31] portrayal, as for instance his handling of Zacchaeus, Nicodemus, the woman at the well, the woman taken in adultery, Peter, Judas, and others. Not arguments, but a relationship in which he gave himself, his respect, acceptance and understanding freely to others. His followers felt the strength of this relationship. They responded to it as far as their own inner conditions permitted. Peter had his struggles. Some wanted to follow but there were too many conflicting demands within them that they could not resolve. Some wanted to control him, but found in his love a strength which would not permit itself to be exploited. Others found in their ability to accept his love the beginning of a new life.

It was this consciousness of his love that led to certain interpretations of the nature and significance of his life, death and resurrection. To be sure, there was a long historical tradition behind these interpretations, but people would never have related Jesus to these traditions had they not felt a reality in their relation to him for which the traditional forms seemed authentic expressions.

One of these interpretations is that of Jesus as the Incarnation of the love of God. This idea is at the heart of the Gospel of John. It is openly expressed in the first chapter, "In the beginning was the Word, and the Word was with God, and the Word was God. . . . And the Word became flesh and dwelt among us, full of grace and truth; we have beheld his glory, glory as of the only Son from the Father." [32] The entire Gospel is an attempt to indicate what this Incarnation meant, not only in theological terms, but in terms of Jesus' relationships with men and women. Here the love of God is made real through living relationships of Jesus with persons like Nicodemus, the woman at the well, the blind man, the woman taken in adultery, the disciples and others. And a major point of this Gospel is that God is love, and that this love is given in grace, that is, without merit. And an almost equally central point is that man finds his truest fulfillment as he painfully learns to respond with love and faith to the love of God.

How do we find strength to follow the teaching of Jesus in regard to loving others? Here we must emphasize our response to the prior love of God. "For God so loved the world that he gave his only Son, that whoever believes in him should not perish but have eternal life." [33] Here the stress is on the prior love of God, but as belief and eternal life are elaborated in the Gospel it is clear that they involve a response of love toward God that expresses itself in love toward man. This idea is pointedly expressed in the Epistle of John: "Beloved, let us love one another; for love is of God, and he who loves is born of God and knows God. He who does not love does not know God; for God is love. In this the love of God was made manifest among us, that God sent his only Son into the world, so that we might live through him. In this is love, not that we loved God but that he loved us and sent his Son to be the expiation for our sins. Beloved, if God so loved us, we also ought to love one another. No man has ever seen God; if we love one another, God abides in us and his love is perfected in us. . . . There is no fear in love, but perfect love casts out fear. . . . We love because he first loved us." [34]

In speaking of love there is always the danger of getting lost in childish sentimentality so that we think of love as a soft, indulgent attitude in God which relieves us of responsibility and makes life easy. Likewise many parents think that to give love to their child is to save him from all effort and suffering. If he does something which hurts another child he is carefully protected from any consequence of his actions. Such attitudes are easily carried up into religion, and God is thought of as a nice old man who pampers his children. Even the will of God can be interpreted to fit our sentimental whim. This is a distortion of the teaching of the New Testament.

At the other extreme there is the problem of human anger and wrath. In anger a parent can punish a child much too severely, and can in this way bring about a feeling of rebellion that leads to more trouble. The parent who is sentimenal about love completely represses his anger because he is afraid of it. The parent who expresses his wrath freely represses his love. Neither helps the child to a realistic understanding of his situation and of the nature of human relationships, and the end results are very much alike.

The Bible is realistic about the nature of God and the nature of life. It does not talk about the love of God without at the same time indicating that the acceptance of this love makes certain demands upon the individual. Throughout the Bible the idea of judgment, of punishment, of the wrath of God is faced.

In relating the wrath of God to the love of God we face the danger of confusing our human feelings with the nature of God. A person who sentimentalizes love will have need to deny the wrath of God. He sees wrath in terms of human anger, and he is right in denying God's wrath in the sense that we should not impute human anger to God. Another projects his feelings of anger on God and becomes a self-appointed dispenser of the wrath of God. In identifying his own anger with that of God he feels justified in punishing others. We may react against such a person or, if we feel deeply guilty, we may accept the punishment such a person has to offer us as a means of atoning for our guilt. Some persons get nothing from a church service if the preacher does not punish them severely; some get little or nothing if the preacher does not punish others but leaves them feeling self-righteous.

The Bible gives deep insight into the problem of God's judgment. God has made man with freedom to accept or reject, to obey or disobey fundamental laws of life, to love or hate, to accept responsibility for himself or refuse it, and to make other such choices. The outcome of each person's life depends in a large part on these choices. Life contains many crises, large and small, which arise because something is wrong in the way we are living, in our real feelings and relationships. Perhaps these crises are manifested in terms of a severe headache or other illness; perhaps they come to light in terms of some failure, or in the eruption of some very unhappy human relationship, or in a gnawing sense of inner discord. They are God's way of confronting us with the realization that we are moving in the wrong direction, and it is time for a realistic appraisal and change within ourselves.

Jesus [35] points up this problem in the parable of the young man who took his possessions and journeyed into a far country. As he sat amid the swine he felt a judgment. He saw where he was in the light of where he could be; what he was in the light of what he could become. The choices were clear. Jesus did not picture God as swinging a club over the boy's head in anger, or sending out a vehement preacher to scold him. The boy came to himself; he judged himself in the light of a more ideal situation, and took the necessary steps to move toward that situation. Here is the judgment of God: that in the life and work of Christ we have an ideal by which we can judge ourselves, and the offer of a relationship with God through which redemption can be experienced. It is ours to accept these opportunities or to suffer from their neglect.

Three other parables give us the insight of Jesus into the problem of judgment and crisis. One [36] is that of the ten maidens who went to meet the bridegroom. Not having enough oil for their lamps five of them wanted to depend on their friends to supply them. But this their friends could not do. So the five foolish maidens missed their opportunity to go into the marriage feast. There is no wasted sentimentality over them; they are out, as many others have been out because of their refusal to meet the necessary conditions which are imposed by the nature of life. While this parable is often interpreted as teaching the need for preparation for the final judgment, its truth is certainly applicable to many other personal situations. We are never permitted to enter into any satisfying experience until we have met conditions necessary for that experience. And there comes a time when it is too late. We cannot live by the insights of others; we must arrive at our own and pay the price for them in terms of struggling with the problems that face us.

Another parable dealing with this matter of judgment and crisis is that of the talents.[37] Here the question asked of each man is simply, What have you done with that which was given you? The man who had not invested his lord's money, but had buried it, found himself cast out. Life and all of its possibilities are gifts; we do not create them. But the outcome of life is bound up with the way in which we use that which was given to us; our abilities, our potentialities and ourselves. Certainly some persons become sick because they have not grown in their capacity to love or in some other aspect of themselves. For some of these there can be cure; for some no cure is possible. Certainly one thing the Bible teaches is the wisdom of learning to use our abilities as they were meant to be used before we lose the power to do so.

A final parable [38] dealing with judgment concerns the coming of the Son of man in his glory, and the separation of the nations as a shepherd separates the sheep from the goats. What is the basis for this judgment? "For I was hungry and you gave me food, I was thirsty and you gave me drink, I was a stranger and you welcomed me, I was naked and you clothed me, I was sick and you visited me, I was in prison and you came to me." When? "As you did it to one of the least of these my brethren, you did it to me." Here the sole basis of judgment is what the person has done to meet the needs of others. To be sensitive to the needs of others, and to give oneself to meeting those needs, is to serve God. Certainly humanity can be divided between those who are sensitive and those who are oblivious to the plight of their fellows. Each of us places himself in one group or the other, and each of these attitudes has a marked influence on the development and outcome of our life.

The fact of experiences which can be described as judgment is not contrary to faith in the love of God. Judgment simply means that there is an underlying moral structure to life, and as one makes choices he places himself under judgment and determines the direction and outcome of his life. God cannot set aside this moral structure. Love offers fellowship out of which comes strength to accept its conditions. But God does not make anyone a special case. Love that is curative or redemptive gives strength to accept basic conditions of life, even when painful or frustrating to childish whims.

It is this fact that man may destroy himself that gives meaning to
the judgment of God. God, if he loves man, must also hate that
which would destroy man. But to take from man his freedom to
choose between that which creates personality and that which
destroys it, is to make man less than man. Man cannot escape the
judgment, pain and suffering involved in his choices. But God also
shares this suffering with him. The wrath of God is not directed to
man, but at that which would destroy man's high possibilities.
This we, ourselves, also should hate.

To state this dilemma from the human point of view, whenever
we are offered a genuine love, either human or divine, we also face
a judgment. What shall we do with this love, accept it or reject it?
In acceptance or rejection, changes take place within us. We feel a
judgment against ourselves in the loss of inner vitality or in the
sense of guilt and worthlessness that follows the rejection of love or
the experience of not being loved. To reject love that is extended
to us is to condemn ourselves.

Jesus stated the great commandment in terms of love. "You shall
love the Lord your God with all your heart, and with all your soul,
and with all your mind. This is the great and first commandment.
And a second is like it, You shall love your neighbor as yourself.
On these two commandments depend all the law and the prophets." [39] These are not to be thought of as commandments which
we can keep by a decision to love or to obey as we might obey a law
governing external actions. Love cannot be ordered. Love can be
given only in response to love. We love because we are first loved;
our learning to love is always a response to love from another. But
we cannot depend on the love of others in any absolute sense, for
they, like us, are not perfect. We can completely trust the love of
God, and in this trust we can learn to love and accept ourselves and
others in spite of imperfections. We can learn, as we understand
God's love for us, to love even our enemies.

Jesus, a man of profound ability to love, asked love of his disciples. "A new commandment I give to you, that you love one another; even as I have loved you, that you also love one another. By
this all men will know that you are my disciples, if you have love

for one another." [40] "This is my commandment, that you love one another as I have loved you. Greater love has no man than this, that a man lay down his life for his friends." [41] Jesus is here using a sound principle of teaching, that of example. As his disciples felt his love for them, they would be moved to love others. This would not be a simple thing for them to do, as they all had attitudes toward others which were adverse to love and would need to be changed. They found it hard to love him when they could not understand his goals. Immature persons ask others to fulfill their expectations as a price for being loved.

What does it mean to love others as oneself? Obviously the meaning is that we should love ourselves. But the Christian Church has often preached against love of self. What does it mean to love oneself?

To love anyone is to be glad that he is alive, to want a full and rich experience for him, to value him as a person so that one respects him and does not exploit him, and to be concerned with his welfare to the point of giving of oneself to meet his needs. In this sense one also needs to love himself. To accept and affirm oneself as a person, to seek a full and rich experience for oneself, to have self-respect, to be concerned for and do what is necessary for our own welfare; these attitudes are necessary to health and well-being. And it is only as we love ourselves in these ways that we can love others. The person who does not respect himself does not respect others; the person who is not concerned about his own welfare cannot be genuinely concerned about the welfare of others. Because we do love others we are under obligation to become the best person possible, for they need us to be our best. A teacher who loves his students will seek to improve himself for their benefit; a physician who loves his patients will seek to become a better physician; a parent who loves his child will seek to become a better person that he might be a better parent. There is nothing in the New Testament which teaches us to impoverish our personalities in order to be helpful or Christian. We are to find the abundant life in order to bring abundance of joy and peace to others. We are to love ourselves so that we may love others as ourselves.

This kind of love of self is to be distinguished from selfishness, or self-centeredness. The selfish person demands that life be organized around him, that he be given to, that others give up their legitimate claims and accept his exorbitant claims, that others permit themselves to be exploited by him. This is not love, or at best is a perverted, infantile kind of love. Neurotic persons are self-centered, and often distort the Christian faith to conform to their attitudes. Much of the preaching against genuine love of self is of this neurotic quality. For the New Testament love means the fulfillment of self that we may give more fully and completely to others. And as we give to others we find fulfillment in ourselves. These two dimensions of experience cannot be separated; they are two sides of a total experience.

There are two great pictures of love in the New Testament. One is a word picture, and it is inspired by the other which is a picture in a life. The word picture is that of Paul in the thirteenth chapter of I Corinthians. The life picture is that of Christ on the Cross. From these two pictures humanity cannot escape, and yet men have never made their full peace with them.

Paul's great poem on love needs to be read, reread and then read again. It is a collection of profound insights by which one can examine his own every-day relationships. The first three verses expose our need to seek excellence on matters of speech, knowledge, faith and the sharing of material possessions in order to compensate for the lack of love in our relationships with others. Here is the reason why so many religious persons lead so impoverished, unhappy and self-defeating lives. Unable to love, they do not seek to get to the root of their problem, but rather attempt to substitute something else for love. But there is no substitute which satisfies the human spirit. The result is emptiness, falseness, nothingness, impoverishment. This impoverishment is likely to turn into a harsh, critical, punishing kind of religion, or an easy, sentimental kind.

The next four verses describe the characteristics of love. Here is a standard by which to measure our own stature. The opposite of these characteristics are immature, neurotic traits with which the psychiatrist is very famiilar. Some honest self-analysis is in the light of these qualities could be helpful, but also difficult.

The final verses contrast the enduring nature of love with the transitory nature of possessions and abilities. There is a perfection about love which these other capacities do not have. That perfection lies in the fact that love as it has been described satisfies man's deepest needs and gives meaning to all other abilities and relationships. This is not the perfectionism of the neurotic who, lacking in love, seeks perfection in terms of external behavior.

In seeking a figure of speech to illustrate his point, Paul seizes upon the analogy of childhood and maturity. The child cannot love in the sense he is describing. To do this, he must give up childish feelings and attitudes and accept more mature attitudes. The description of mature love offered by many psychiatrists is strangly similar to that of Paul.

There is an insight in these final verses which is often passed over. As we arrive at the realization of our ability to love we come to understand ourselves. Love and self-understanding do go together. But also we understand fully as first we have been fully understood. Understood by whom? Perhaps by other persons. But a unique aspect of the Christian faith is this consciousness of God's prior love and understanding as revealed in the person of Christ. This love and understanding operates through human relationships; if we are not understood we find it very difficult to understand. And when we come to understand we find it is through a relationship in which we have been understood. Such a relationship is the expression of the life of God in man, whether man be conscious of this fact or not. Therefore love abides, since God is love.

The great picture of love in the New Testament is that of Christ on the Cross.[42] Here in the midst of intense suffering inflicted on him by persons driven by anxiety and hate, Christ prayed for the forgiveness of those who slew him through their own anxiety and hate. Jesus here shows the tremendous capacity of love to absorb hate without passing it on or dealing it back. He understands the blindness of his executioners; they do not know what they do. He has no desire to punish them; he rather desires their redemption.

Here is an act which appeals to man's deepest impulses and reason, but one which each person must take into himself in order for it to do its work on him.

Realizing what kind of creatures we are, we would turn from such overwhelming love except that we sense Christ's identification of himself with us to the extent that we are able to identify ourselves with him. In our anxiety we can know that there is no depth that he has not plumbed. Yet he did not stay there. In absorbing hate he felt himself cut off even from God,[43] but in the midst of this separation he finds a strengthening, binding faith. The God in whom we have faith in hours of ease may not be the same God as we find in hours of pain; there we need a greater, stronger God. So Christ could cut through his sense of separation and find his faith again, "Father, into thy hands I commit my spirit." [44] To him the love of God was stronger than his pain.

Here, then, is part of the meaning of the Cross. Through the profound level of love and faith which Jesus demonstrated in the midst of terrible suffering, the Cross has come to symbolize a way of hope and victory over the suffering of separation and guilt. It does not speak of the suffering which we bring on ourselves for the sake of punishment. This suffering must be mastered through outgrowing the need for self-punishment or the desire for martyrdom. The Cross does speak of the kind of suffering which comes from having our love rejected or from the guilt of having rejected love. It says that the final answer to both rejection and guilt is a love that is strong enough to bridge the separation which rejection and guilt create. It is such a love that has the power to reach through anxiety and guilt and bring belonging, forgiveness and redemption.

This interpretation removes the element of magic from the Cross. So many, having failed to grow to the level of love which we see there, revert back to a more childish belief that somehow the Cross will change us in some miraculous fashion, without any responsibility on our part. This attitude involves a distorted view of ourselves, of life and of the New Testament faith. And it leaves many disillusioned.

The emphasis on the miraculous is distorted because it is one-sided. There is no question of our need for receptivity. No man is sufficient unto himself; he must receive from others and from God. To receive from others is to receive from God, for no one could give without a basic structure in life which makes such giving possible and satisfying. But the one who receives must at the same time also give of himself. This outgoing is necessary to receiving. And this giving of himself involves changing himself, in a measure, toward the likeness of the one from whom he receives. And when the one from whom he receives enjoins him to become himself, as genuine love does, then he is free to grow toward the fulfillment of his own nature. The Christian faith holds that there is a profound harmony between man's true nature and the nature of God.

Any experience in which we receive love in the sense of a union or belonging that overcomes our separateness may speak to us of the love of God. Such experiences may be accepted as a sacrament which speaks of a love which undergirds all of life. And our responses are as though we were responding to the love of God, when we see life in this sacramental sense. The task of the pastor and of the entire fellowship of the church is to bring such love to others, and thus make real the love of God. "Be kind to one another, tenderhearted, forgiving one another, as God in Christ forgave you." [45]

The way in which the love of God becomes most real in human life is through the life and work of Christ. Here we see a uniting, reconciling kind of love which reaches beneath human guilt and separation and gives those who can realize its meaning a sense of profound belonging in the universe and to God. Here is a work of reconciliation akin to but far deeper and more trustworthy than what we find on the strictly human level. The human may speak to us of the divine love; it is an expression of and promise of the larger love out of which it grows. The love of God speaks to us of the profound possibilities of love toward God and toward our fellow men. It is the groundwork and foundation for a sense of community, one of the necessary conditions for the healthy functioning of the person and of the group. It is a profound source of strength for those inevitable experiences of illness which threaten existence itself. In the realization of the love of God as revealed in Christ many have found a peace out of which comes strength to meet the various strains and stresses of existence.

## Chapter Five

# The Healing Fellowship

THE INFLUENCE of our personal relationships on our health is sometimes obvious; sometimes subtle and difficult to understand, as we have seen. Therefore the actual diagnosis of specific illness in terms of emotional factors involved should be left to experts in this field. Certainly we should not probe into the emotional conflicts of our friends when they become ill.

Identification is one psychological process through which our relationships with others influences our growth and health. This is a deep, unconscious process which the average person often confuses with imitation. Imitation is just aping someone, consciously intending to do what others do. Identification is a deeper, emotional process through which we seek to become like another person in attitudes, feelings and hence behavior, by taking something of the other person into ourselves. The little boy, for example, identifies with his father and wants to do what he does; he intends to be a doctor, or whatever, like the father. The little girl takes to her dolls and gives them good care when mother has a new baby. While the child's first identifications are with his parents, as he gets older he identifies with teachers, policemen, scout leaders, other children, the pastor and many others.

But identification goes a step beyond individuals; we also identify with groups. Every child goes through a stage when the edicts of the group about such things as clothes and hours is much more important to him than the edicts of his parents. He wants to belong to the group and to do this he feels he must be like them. However, this sort of identification does not mean that he will grow up to be a hopeless conformist. If his growth is healthy, a day will come when he will feel strong enough to express his individuality, but he will express himself in a way which contributes to the group rather than merely conforming to or interfering with it. In adult life the conformist is motivated by anxiety; he has to conform out of fear, while the rabid nonconformist is likely to be motivated by hostility; he feels compelled to force his way on the group.

The need for belonging is realized through this ability to identify with other individuals and with groups. The child of eight to ten wants to belong to groups and do things in groups of his own age. The adolescent is strongly motivated by what the group thinks. The adult also needs groups in order to maintain his emotional and spiritual health. At the very time in our culture when family ties appear to be weakening, there is a veritable flood of groups to which we may belong. Almost any cause or interest can be a point around which to organize a group. Some persons are so involved in groups that they have no time to develop the relationships they need to their primary group, the family. Or perhaps it is more accurate to say that they feel unable to find closeness, warmth and belonging in the family group, and therefore they seek it in other groups. When we are cut off from groups emotionally, or when we cut ourselves off, we feel lost. Some forms of mental illness are characterized by an extreme sense of isolation, and the assurance of acceptance can be a very helpful means of recovery.

In identifying with groups we find meaning which gives our lives stability and continuity. Groups, such as the family, church, school or nation, define for us the kind of a person we should be, and place pressures on us to achieve their ideals. They not only give us status and importance, but also an external standard by which to judge ourselves.

The extent to which we identify with groups can be seen in the way in which we talk about them—"my church," "my club," "my outfit," "my school." Sometimes our reliance on groups and our loyalty to them reflect a childishness which is unhealthy in adult life. Leaders at times foster this childish loyalty as a means of maintaining their power. But the emotionally and spiritually healthy adult also wants to belong to groups. In this he exercises independent thought and judgment, and a desire to be helpful as well as to find help. The mature leader does not seek to dominate his group, but to help the group find the satisfaction of its needs. In this he finds his own satisfactions.

It is no accident that the faith expressed in the Bible places a strong emphasis on the relation of the individual to the group. Vital religious faith does not see the individual apart from others and from God; it sees all in a total relationship. Thus while redemption is always a personal matter, it takes place in and through a society of persons who are experiencing a common faith. This society is the Christian community. While the psychologist describes the needs of persons and indicates how they are satisfied or frustrated in group relationships, the Christian faith offers a creative experience in which the individual finds acceptance and fellowship through the Church. Identification takes place here, as through the fellowship the person finds elements of strength and direction, and in turn learns to contribute to the purposes of the group. In this experience of Christian fellowship God is at work, and the Bible interprets this as the activity of the Holy Spirit. The church of the New Testament was a group in which the members found this deep sense of belonging or community with their fellow Christians.

The problems of health cannot be adequately discussed without dealing with the experience of community and fellowship as recorded in the Bible. Anxiety is often the result of broken community; faith means trust in others and this creates and sustains community even as community contributes to faith. Hate destroys fellowship, except when it can be openly confessed and accepted; then it leads to love and understanding. Sin is a condition of separation; forgiveness restores fellowship. Free and open communication is necessary for community, and in its highest expression community issues in that depth of understanding which we call communion.

The experience of community is a large and important theme in the New Testament, and it is undergoing considerable study at the present time.[1] It is of central significance for the relation of religion to health. The Bible speaks of the saving, redemptive fellowship; of the believing fellowship; of the worshiping fellowship; and of the serving fellowship.

## The Redemptive Fellowship

In the New Testament the saving or redemptive fellowship is an expression of the life and work of Christ as experienced by his followers. Jesus was a master at breaking through feelings of isolation and giving persons a feeling of acceptance and understanding. This was not a matter of easy technique, but rather of genuine and profound love and compassion. His ability to feel the suffering of others led to insight into their needs. He had a great capacity for giving himself to others. Our modern emphasis on techniques of human relations is an expression of our failure to find the deeper and genuine basis of creative human relations.

One illustration of Jesus' sensitivity to the needs of others and his capacity to reach out to them at the point of their need is to be found in his experience with Zacchaeus.[2] Here the inferior, ostracized little man up a tree became the object of his attention, and the kind of fellowship which Jesus offered became a redemptive influence in his life. Again in his relationship with the woman at the well,[3] Jesus was able to offer a sufficiently strong sense of acceptance so that they were able to get beneath superficial, but separating, questions of religion to deeper issues of life. His dealing with the woman taken in adultery[4] shows his use of acceptance and forgiveness to restore broken relationships. The sick man who was let down through the roof[5] found healing through an experience of forgiveness.

It is this kind of restoration to wholeness to which the rest of the New Testament bears witness. Throughout there is stress on the idea that Christian experience is a joint possession which each Christian has in common with all others and which binds them together in a fellowship. Paul has many phrases which express this idea; "participation in the Spirit," "being of the same mind, having the same love, being in full accord and of one mind," [6] "partnership in the gospel," [7] and "the fellowship of the Holy Spirit." [8] Writing to the Roman Christians he points out that Christians, though many, are really "one body in Christ, and individually members one of another." [9] And this theme is elaborated in his first letter to the Corinthians where he goes into detail to show how the whole body is dependent on the functions of each member or organ, and to compare the Church with the body of Christ. "You are the body of Christ and individually members of it." [10] The more excellent way, the way in which this body will function at its highest level of creativity and redemptive power, is for each member to be able to relate to the other members in terms of the love which he then describes. The twelfth and thirteenth chapters should be read together.

There are two dimensions in this experience of Christian community. One expresses their relationship with Christ; in Christ all share a common good, and this is redemption. No man redeems himself, he is redeemed by Christ. His followers participate in this common life, they partake a common Cup, they are empowered by the same Spirit, they have a common hope. The emphasis is on an active relationship with Christ as the Head, from whom they have all received.

The other dimension expresses the relationship they bear with one another through sharing in the redemptive work of Christ. Participation in a common salvation makes them brothers. Apostles, prophets, teachers, healers—each in his own way and with whatever gifts he has received makes his contribution to the community of Christians. Each has a responsibility to the others, but this responsibility is not motivated by legalistic requirements, but by freedom in the kind of love which creates mutual helpfulness. These dimensions of Christian experience are organically related.

When we turn to the interpretation of Christian experience as found in the writings attributed to John, we find this same sense of belonging to God and through God to one another. In the First Letter of John, the author states that he is proclaiming the life which he saw in Christ "so that you may have fellowship with us; and our fellowship is with the Father and with his Son Jesus Christ." [11] In the Fourth Gospel this relationship is interpreted through the figure of the vine and the branches, Christ being the vine and Christians being the branches in an organic relationship with the vine and hence with one another.[12] It is made more specific in terms of love: "A new commandment I give to you, that you love one another; even as I have loved you, that you also love one another. By this all men will know that you are my disciples, if you have love for one another." [13] In the very moving prayer which is recorded as coming from the lips of Jesus we find the words, "I do not pray for these only, but also for those who are to believe in me through their word, that they may all be one; even as thou, Father, art in me, and I in thee, that they also may be in us, so that the world may believe that thou hast sent me." [14]

It would be difficult to find figures of speech which more vividly communicate the profound experience of participation and community. Words are inadequate to express fully such realities which are inward and intangible, though terribly real and powerful. In Christian experience participation in the life of God centers in the love of God as it was revealed in Christ, love which redeems men as persons, and makes them aware of their brotherhood, their oneness and unity, but also of their individuality as Sons. The New Testament does not teach that men should become so absorbed in God nor in conformity to a group that they lose their identity as persons. Rather they find completion of their personal identity through participation in the life of God and of their fellow men. This is a positive contribution to both health and spiritual wholeness.

This capacity for belonging and participation is potentially inherent in each person. But it must be actualized in experience; it cannot be passed on verbally. This is the great task of the Church today—to bring persons of all ages into this experience of fellowship and to lead them into the kind of participation in the life of God and in the lives of their fellow men that makes redemption a reality. This is the reason that Christian love is important in the sense of giving oneself to meet the needs of one's neighbor; it is essential to community. But we cannot give such love until we have received it from others and understand it in the light of God's love. Out of a deep sense of gratitude for what we have received we find ourselves moved to give. Part of our giving lies in renunciation of whatever in ourselves would hurt others; part in terms of a commitment to positive actions which serve the needs of others. In this experience there is no place for legalism which forces one to obey a code of behavior out of fear.

Obviously feelings of anxiety, guilt and hate grow out of a lack of belonging and in turn create further barriers to belonging. They make communication difficult or impossible, so that even though people try to talk they do not mean the same thing by their words and hence there is no real communication, consequently no sense of communion. Communion depends on our ability to share ourselves with others, and for many in our culture sharing things is much easier than sharing oneself.

There are then two basic conditions under which man may live. One is described by the words community, belonging and fellowship; the other is described by isolation, estrangement and aloneness. There are various degrees of these conditions and most of us have experienced them all at various times. Fellowship is essential for health; isolation leads to illness in one form or another. In fostering the experience of Christian community the Church provides a foundation for the development of wholesome, mature persons and the prevention of much illness, hence becoming a powerful healing force in society.

In speaking of healing, two processes need to be distinguished. One operates on the level of our relationship to a group in which we find either those satisfactions or those conflicts which affect health. The other process operates on the level of life structure, either organic structure or psychological, which results from the habitual ways in which we respond to anxiety-producing relationships. In the case of stomach ulcer there is an actual organic change in the stomach, whether from a physical or emotional cause. Likewise the delusions of a mentally ill person become a psychological structure which expresses and at the same time supports and confirms faulty relationships.

Now the total process of healing requires that each of these levels be taken into account. The physician who treats physical illnesses may be primarily concerned with altering the structure and functioning of a given organ. He may or may not be aware of, or interested in, the problem of the patient's relationships. The psychiatrist who is primarily interested in psychotherapy is very much concerned with the patient's relationships, though he is also concerned with structural changes within the patient's body. The pastor, representing religion, is primarily concerned with the problem of relationships and secondarily concerned with organic processes. He may help a person with a sense of guilt, but he is not in any position to treat a structural change which that guilt may have created.

These conditions have implications both for religious and medical healing. The weakness and futility of much "faith" healing lies in leaving the entire structural side of life out of consideration. Some such healing is also grounded in such a distorted view of reality and of the true nature of faith that it does much more harm than good. On the other hand, that medical healing which leaves out of consideration the emotional and spiritual life of the patient is not adequate and at times may be harmful, for it may heal the patient's body, while leaving deeper illness untouched. Or it may help a patient to escape from a deeper illness by refuge in physical symptoms which cannot be cured.

All of these limitations add up to the fact that it is difficult for any professional worker to maintain a comprehensive view of life and of the problems of illness and health. By virtue of our tasks we all tend to become specialists. But being specialists does not mean that we must be separated and deny reality to other points of view. For the sake of the patient we, the healing team, need to belong to one another. And other healers, such as psychologists and social workers, should be included in the team, for it is only through a fellowship of healers that the whole patient will find healing. Such a fellowship is part of the Christian enterprise. Church-related hospitals should be among the leaders in this area.

In regard to the work of the pastor, one further observation may be made. The pastor, as the leader of the fellowship, has a major opportunity in promoting this sense of community. Through his relationships with his people he can help them to feel accepted or unacceptable, in fellowship or isolated. The kind of relationships which he as a person creates will be a symbol to his people of the kind of relationship which God offers them. He can mediate to them something of the love of God, or something of fear and divisiveness. And a pastor who has achieved in himself the confidence of wholeness will help his church to become whole.

One of the tasks of the modern pastor which is taking on increasing significance is that of pastoral counseling. The basic principle here is not new. The value of confession is clear in the New Testament,[15] and before, but for various reasons it has been allowed to recede into the background in our Protestant churches. However, it is again coming to the fore, partly because of the interest of pastors and partly because of the sheer need of people to unburden themselves and find help.

How does pastoral counseling serve the needs of community? The pastoral counselor spends much time with individuals; he does not have time to see great numbers. But with those he does see his work, if effective, goes deep. It can involve a radical change in attitudes, feelings and relationships. The problems which come to the pastor are basically those of relationships which in one way or another are broken and need restoration. A mother alienated from her son, a son alienated from both of his parents, a young woman caught in a conflict between her parents, husband and wife working out their hostilities on each other, a young man trying to break away from a hostile, cruel father, a young woman trying to break away from possessive parents, young people all mixed up about their various sexual attitudes—all basically problems of broken relationships. When the pastor helps one person he is helping many others. People are not really helped unless they are able to have more understanding, loving, trusting relationships with others. Indeed, one of the functions of pastoral counseling is helping to remove barriers to fellowship, and thus in a real way creating a sense of Christian community.

## The Believing Community

While the Christian community is one in which fellowship and belonging are experienced redemptively, it is also a believing community.

Believing is related to anxiety and faith in a direct manner, for in the New Testament faith and believing express the same experience, that of such a profound trust in another person, primarily in Christ, that there is a complete giving of oneself in commitment. To believe is not just to hold a particular, intellectual opinion. It is a dynamic expression of the whole person, not a static formulation in so many words. The Christian community is a group whose basic relationship to God and to one another is one of trustful commitment. This community has some beliefs, such as the Lordship of Christ. What is the relationship between beliefs, believing and health?

One of the gifts which distinguish man from all other animals is the capacity to become aware of his experience and to formulate its meaning in intellectual symbols through which he may communicate with others. The experience itself is never communicated; the symbol becomes a bridge which reaches into the mind of another and calls into his awareness a corresponding meaning. The words "I love you" may mean one thing to the speaker and another to the person spoken to, or they may mean the same to each. If they have different meanings there is inadequate communication and hence no deep sense of closeness; if they have the same meaning there is real communication and communion. The Apostles' Creed, an ancient formulation of Christian belief, is not real to many modern Christians, that is, it does not convey any meaning. This may be because the words themselves are unfamiliar to us, or not vital in our thinking. Or it may be because we lack the essential inner experience which these words are seeking to express and communicate. The creed or belief never creates the experience. Christian experience is the result of our relationship with God in Christ and with our fellow men; creeds may express and communicate it, they may point to it, but never create it.

The basic purpose of this capacity for formulation and communication seems to be that of bringing insight or understanding into the awareness of the individual and the group. On the basis of conscious understanding of the dynamic factors that are deep in our human relationships, the life of the individual within the group may be evaluated. It is through communicating our inner experience to another in an atmosphere of acceptance and understanding that insight grows. Any real sense of community among individuals is dependent on certain common experiences and insights which are formulated into commonly accepted beliefs. These beliefs serve as a binding force, making for wholeness within the individual and within the community.

But beliefs are subject to distortion by either the individual or the group. This distortion occurs when attention is concentrated on the belief itself, rather than on the realities of interpersonal relationships which it seeks to express. In this situation beliefs themselves become important, not the living process of believing. The real, inner meaning of experience is concealed from consciousness, primarily because it is painful. Growth and wholeness come only through the process of allowing experience to reveal its meaning to us. Revelation is the action of God in communicating through the realities of human experience. Insight is the human side of this process; we see into the meaning that experience is revealing to us.

To take a very simple formulation of believing or trusting as an illustration: "God is good." This declaration simply asserts that we find in our experience a reality on which we are dependent and that this reality is essentially of a nature which seeks the fulfillment of human life. Now we can believe that God is good simply because someone, or a group, tells us so. Here we believe because someone in whom we have confidence, or with whom for some reason we need to conform, assures us that this is true. But if our own experience in human relationships has been painful, and if we strongly fear that others will hurt us, we may not be able to accept this declaration in any vital sense. But we may still accept it superficially, pushing back our own feelings because we also feel a need to belong to the group and believe what they believe. If, then, we meet a misfortune or become ill, we are very likely to revert to our deeper feeling that God is not good, else why should we suffer?

Or we may choose a different reaction, and deny that God is good, tell the group that it is wrong and find ourselves in a state of rebellion. Here also we will feel isolated from the group, but our rebellion may be strong enough to formulate a very elaborate anti-group philosophy which we consider to be the truth. Because others have had a similar kind of experience, they may agree with our ideas, and this reinforces our conviction of their truth.

There is another thing we may do. We may feel the difference between the group's ideas and our own experience, and we may set about to discover why we feel as we do. But to do this we must have a relationship with a person or persons which is essentially good in the sense that it affirms and assists our need for growth and self-fulfillment. Here is the crux of the problem in so far as the group is concerned. If we are members of a church which is concerned primarily to have us believe the formula, God is good, and which uses various techniques of coercion to get us to accept it, then we have little chance to get at the deeper roots of our painful feelings. But if we are members of a church which is more concerned with giving us a good experience, that is, a sense of fellowship and belonging that gives meaning to the words, God is good, then we have a chance for outgrowing our painful experiences and finding a greater fulfillment. Here the church becomes a source of revelation; our inner processes in understanding this experience become a source of insight. The tragedy is that too many churches are concerned more with the formulation than with the experience.

Now if we happen to be persons who are emotionally immature to whom the word "good" means that we are given everything we want, and no demands are made upon us; if we expect to receive without giving anything in return, then God is good only as long as we are getting what we want and are required to make no positive response. But this is not the nature of life, as modern psychology is very quick to remind us. For life does involve struggle, conflict, pain, suffering. The Christian faith has long known this fact also.

Mature Christian experience requires much more than a belief in any set of words. It involves a living relationship with other persons and with God in Christ through which we find strength to face and accept painful reality and to respond in love and trust. This requires giving up our childish insistence that life be "happy"; giving up any desire to suffer for the sake of suffering and getting sympathy; being willing to face and resolve those painful elements in our experience which can be resolved; and learning to live constructively with those elements which cannot be resolved. In so far as a church helps us to do this, it is contributing to the maturing and fulfillment of our personalities, and helping us to attain genuine wholeness.

There are certain external marks of unhealthy use of beliefs. One is that we feel we must be very aggressive in forcing others to accept our formulations. This kind of force is quite different from the strength which comes from genuine love and trust. It is born out of anxiety, guilt or hostility, or a combination of these feelings. It may drive us to certain superficial achievements, even to starting a new religious cult, but it will not make us genuinely whole.

When beliefs are used in an unhealthy fashion they become rigid, well crystallized, and overdeveloped intellectually. Our security is found in our ideas and we do not want to be disturbed by any question as to what our ideas really mean. Therefore we become defensive, and are disturbed when anyone questions us. We consider doubt a grave sin, since it challenges us to look more deeply into ourselves. Overdevelopment of our beliefs intellectually is part of our desire to defend them; if we can prove them to others then we are right. This exaggerated need to be right also gives us a false sense of security; it is as though we felt, If I have the truth I am safe, no one can hurt me, and I do not have to be concerned about my personal relationships.

Jesus did not give us any formulated creed or set of beliefs; he presented a living, growing relationship between God and man, man and God, and man and himself through which the abundant life was to be achieved. And it was a relationship which led to the mastery of evil and suffering. He had his difficulties with those who found a false security in rigid beliefs into which others were to be coerced.[16] The conversion of Saul of Tarsus was essentially one from security in authoritative beliefs and codes to the deeper experience of spontaneous trust and love from which real strength and growth came. His conversion experience was the beginning of growth, and his letters reveal the struggle which he had in becoming mature in faith and love.

The real Christian community is not, then, one founded on rigid formulations, but one founded on relationships of mutual trust and love. Here love is to be thought of in terms of the self-giving of God to man, and man's response by showing a measure of this self-giving to his fellow men. In this mutual experience of receiving and giving come fulfillment, health and wholeness.

This is the basic meaning of John 3:16, "For God so loved the world that. . . ." Here the word "believe" occurs, but it is belief in terms of trusting deeply, not just accepting a verbal formula. Believing always means trust in the Gospel of John. It is a verb, not a noun. It expresses a process which is dynamic and continuing. So we read, "But to all who received him, who believed in his name, he gave power to become children of God." [17] Here the word "believe" is related to the idea of receptivity and acceptance as an initial step, and it leads to power, that is, strength and wholeness. We also see some of the dynamics of believing in the experience of the man born blind.[18] On the basis of his experience with Jesus he could do nothing but believe on him even in the face of a threat from the critics of Jesus. In this experience there is the suggestion of a relationship between believing and sight, not physical sight, but a seeing into the nature of one's experience to understand its meaning. This capacity for insight certainly involves being able to recognize those whom one can trust.

It is this living experience of faith and trust which unites us as members of the Christian community, as members of the body of Christ, as brothers, fellow pilgrims, a living organic whole. This is definitely the emphasis of Paul in I Corinthians 12, where the Christian community is likened to the body, having many members but each contributing its particular function to the welfare of the whole. The eleventh chapter of Hebrews gives a sense of continuity to this community, and emphasizes that it is a community of faith which resulted in achievements.

Now a church can be founded on the basis of rigid, authoritarian beliefs which members accept because they are presented authoritatively as the way of salvation. It is said that many people in our culture need such authoritarian coercion. The fact that so many persons accept and seek to follow groups which operate on this basis is evidence of the immaturities in our culture. The same needs find expression in political and social beliefs. Many, seeking freedom from authoritarian churches, have found that some liberal churches had little to offer them for their daily existence. The liberal churches have a profound opportunity to make a contribution to growth, health and salvation by offering the security of Christian fellowship rather than the security of rigid beliefs, and the opportunity for full self-expression in Christian living rather than authoritarian moral codes. It is significant that Jesus, in dealing with questions of judgment, did not ask what beliefs a person held. He did ask, What have you done with that which was given you? And, Did you show compassion to your fellow sufferers? [19]

There are elements within every person who seeks membership in the Christian community which work against that fellowship. Belonging in such a group does not automatically remove habitually destructive ways of expressing hostilities or fears or jealousies. Anyone who takes the Christian faith seriously soon becomes aware of difficulties. But to take the faith seriously means to seek to work out these problems; it does not mean to change the faith in order to justify the expression of our particular impulses. The world expects Christians to become saints automatically, and is quick to hurl the charge of hypocrisy as a defense against its own guilt. But the saint is not one who is perfect; he is very much aware of his imperfections. He is seeking a relationship with God which enables him to deal with his weakness in a way that his harm to others is decreased and his helpfulness increased.

The Christian Church has had to devise ways of dealing with this problem of conflict within the Christian community and of re-establishing fellowship. Sometimes it has tried to do this by the reassertion and reinforcement of beliefs, even burning heretics at the stake. This kind of persecution occurs when leaders themselves are very anxious and hostile.

The Church has also developed ways of re-establishing the fellowship which are grounded in trust and love, involving confession, repentance and forgiveness. To be sure, these ways can be administered in a coercive, authoritarian manner, but essentially they are relationships which express trust, acceptance and compassion, and are essential for the continuing life of the Christian community. Where anxiety, guilt and hostility are buried, in persons or groups, sooner or later there will be disintegration in one form or another. Confession, repentance, forgiveness and the re-establishment of a sense of belonging are essential to wholeness.

What can we trust? In whom can we believe? One often hears these questions asked. But a deeper question is, What is influencing the form and nature of our beliefs? Why do we believe as we do? Why do we have doubts? Why do certain beliefs seem unreal to us, and why do others seem so real and important that we will fight for them?

Belief, as has been suggested previously, is a formulation of the meaning and value of experience. Beliefs are statements of the way we perceive life, how it looks to us, what we find is valuable and important. These interpretations in turn depend a great deal on our feelings. When we are anxious we are very likely to formulate beliefs that express and justify that anxiety. An angry man can believe certain things about his wife which he cannot possibly believe when he gets over his anger. On the other hand, our perception of the meaning and value of our experience may be guided by trust and love. Then our beliefs may have an entirely different quality and may change greatly in content. And our beliefs may be grounded in strong feelings of which we are not aware.

Our problem then is not only what we believe but why? This is the kind of insight which we need. There is a point beyond which reason cannot go in validating our deeper convictions about life.

Beyond this limit faith becomes the validating aspect of experience. But faith is always grounded in love. The task of the Christian community is that of giving its members relationships of love, acceptance, understanding, freedom and responsibiilty so that in the growth of persons Christian insights may find their deepest validation. For Christian truth is not a static belief which can be formulated once and for all. It is a dynamic power within human relationships which must be demonstrated daily and hourly. Our basic problem is to get behind our beliefs to the motivation out of which they spring. The more mature and loving we are in the sense of self-giving, the better we are qualified to understand the nature of the realities of human life and religious experience.

The Christian community is a fellowship of believers who have not arrived at perfection. It is a Community-in-search-and-in-growth under allegiance to Christ. Its members do not necessarily hold to the same theology or creed; but in love and trust they share together in the kind of human relationships which promote growth and health. It is not a community which has founded itself, but it has a deep sense that it has been found of God, and in this faith it moves toward a greater realization of its potentiality. "So then you are no longer strangers and sojourners, but you are fellow citizens with the saints and members of the household of God, built upon the foundation of the apostles and prophets, Christ Jesus himself being the chief cornerstone, in whom the whole structure is joined together and grows into a holy temple in the Lord; in whom you also are built into it for a dwelling place of God in the Spirit." [20]

## The Worshiping Community

The Christian community is a worshiping community. Indeed, worship is the unique characteristic of any religious community. In the Old Testament, the Temple was the center of Jewish community and life. In the early Christian community worship was central. Today the church and synagogue preserve and promote the worship of God; remove worship from the religious community and it ceases to be religious.

When we ask about the relation of worship to problems of illness and health we get into a veritable maze of difficulties. Worship is such an inward, personal experience that it is difficult to study. The extreme opinions range from those persons who see absolutely no value in worship to those who feel that through worship and prayer almost any illness may be cured. Here we shall try to discuss some of the factors which bear on this problem.

There is no other human experience which so uniquely combines elements of man's inner world with man's external world as does worship. The central object in genuine Christian worship is God as he is in Christ. God here is a being who loves in the sense of desiring the fulfillment of his creation and of being willing to give himself completely to this end. The fact that man can worship is a gift of God, not only in the sense of man's being created so that worship is within his power, but also in the sense of an understanding of God in the Christian revelation which makes worship possible and desirable for man. God is worthy of man's worship; man feels called to respond with love, adoration, praise, confession, self-giving. These are ways of creating and developing the human side of man's relationship with God. And through this relationship man himself grows.

But what "God" means to each of us is not determined solely, or sometimes even primarily, by the Christian revelation. It is determined by feelings, attitudes and relationships which we have had with significant persons in our early experiences, persons to whom in our childhood we ascribed the characteristics of omnipotence and omniscience or who exercised authority over us or love toward us. When there has been fear, guilt, hostility in relationship to such persons, which has not been outgrown, there is likely to be a similar response to God when one moves toward the experience of worship. There are persons who find themselves very frightened or disturbed by anger in the midst of a Christian worship service when the idea of God as father is expressed. Others may have had such feelings, but were able to keep them out of consciousness. Still others may respond with a feeling of trust and commitment. The experience of worship attempts to make the meaning of God in the Christian sense real and actual, and each worshiper responds with whatever feelings and attitudes he has previously developed in connection with such meanings and symbols.

Real worship thus presents serious difficulties to modern man, and when these difficulties are understood it can be seen why so many avoid worship, and why others turn it into an empty form. In order to worship, to grasp the meaning of God in the Christian sense, and to make an appropriate emotional, intellectual and volitional response to that meaning, each person must face and work through the emotional obstacles within himself. Worship, when it is a living experience, brings the worshiper face to face with himself in the light of the God that is real to him. It may make him aware of potentialities which he would like to avoid, since acceptance of them incurs responsibility to use them. It may make him aware of weaknesses and sins which he would like to cover up because they are painful to admit. Man is never so much in danger nor so near to finding his real self as when he becomes aware of the God who seeks his complete fulfillment.

Worship may serve a unique purpose by helping a person to grow into an identification with the Ultimate Source of his being. In identifying with other persons we keep our relationship on the level of finite beings like unto ourselves in both strength and weaknesses. In identifying with God-in-Christ we look out beyond the human, finite level to the infinite Ground and Source of life itself. But we cannot do this without at the same time dealing with our identifications on the human level wherever these identifications are in conflict. For God is not just our God, he is the God of all men and love of our fellow men is one way that we express our love toward God. Modern psychology has confirmed the insight that our attitude toward others is the same as our attitudes toward ourselves; if we love ourselves we will love others; if we fear or reject ourselves we will fear or reject others. This same principle holds in our relationship with God.

A question may be raised in regard to our identification with God or Christ. Is not God so far removed from us in majesty and holiness that any experience of identification analogous to identification with our fellow men is impossible? Not if the revelation of God in

Christ has truth in it. For in this revelation the transcendental majesty and holiness of God is balanced by the Incarnation of God in Christ. "The Word became flesh and dwelt among us," as we read in the Prologue of the Gospel of John. To dwell, as some do, on the transcendental holiness and majesty of God in a way which emphasizes man's alienation is to foster an unhealthy attitude. There is no redemption here. On the other hand, to identify God with ourselves completely as some mentally ill persons do when they believe they are God, is to seek to escape from a deep sense of alienation by denying it in inflating our ego to cosmic proportions. To preserve a sense of God's majesty and holiness while at the same time finding an identity with him in which our own integrity as a person and our sense of our human brotherhood is strengthened, is the core of Christian experience. This is the goal of the life and ministry of Jesus, which flowers in a redemptive, believing and worshiping community.

Real worship then leads to insight into ourselves and the kind of relationships we have with ourselves and with others and with God. The acts of adoration, confession and dedication require the creating and establishing of Christian relationships with our fellow men. This requirement is expressed in the words of Jesus: "If you are offering your gift at the altar, and there remember that your brother has something against you, leave your gift there before the altar and go; first be reconciled to your brother, and then come and offer your gift." [21] Some persons find it necessary to go through a counseling experience or a psychotherapeutic experience in order to free themselves from intense antagonisms toward others before they find worship possible. Under some conditions others find such growth taking place through worship itself.

Real worship then involves facing oneself in his relationships with others and with God. At times this is a painful experience and at times it is joyous. At times it is disturbing and at times comforting. At times it is upsetting and at times it brings peace. At times it seems very frustrating, and at times it is very satisfying. At times it seems to leave one confused, and at other times the vision and purpose of life are clarified. Whatever happens in a given experience of worship is indicative of the inner condition of the worshiper. To strive for a particular goal such as peace of mind is a false method of worship. Peace of mind may come, but it will come because one has gained some new insights into himself and his relationships and has moved toward the resolution of some conflicts or the strengthening of some positive aspect of his life. Before growth of this kind occurs the person may become more aware of conflict and of the difficulty in making the kind of a decision which promotes growth.

Worship, in the Christian sense, is fundamentally an experience of fellowship or community. This is the nature of the relationship which God offers to man—a reconciliation, a sense of belonging, an experience of worth as a human being. Man's response in terms of acceptance of forgiveness, in terms of a willingness to co-operate with the purposes of God as they are revealed in his own life—these experiences establish a sense of fellowship. The group is inevitably involved in these experiences, for though a person may worship in physical isolation, his relationships with others are never resolved nor set aside by mere physical separation. In group worship the individual's sense of relationship is emphasized and intensified. A sense of togetherness may be created here which surpasses that created in most other kinds of experiences. Indeed, it may reach out and give meaning to other kinds of experiences. In worship one may come to sense that his fears, guilts, hates, loves, ambitions, hopes and faiths are common to and shared by his fellow men. He may come not only to a knowledge of himself but of others, and it is a kind of knowledge that forms a community of sympathy and support, and which binds persons together in common purposes. Worship creates a sense of Christian community, and a sense of Christian community in turn leads the group toward worship.

The influence of worship on health involves a paradox. Real worship does produce values, attitudes, feelings, decisons, which may have a very favorable effect on the functionings of one's body or mind. In some persons it may release guilt which is causing some kind of illness. But to strive for a result like the removal of symptoms through worship is to miss the fundamental character of worship. Worship cannot be made a utilitarian affair without destroying its fundamental nature. For Christian worship is an experience through which man relates himself to God as he is revealed in Christ. It is not an experience in which man may relate God to himself. To use worship in a utilitarian sense, to get what I want, is to seek to do what cannot be done, namely, manipulate God. The dominant mood of Christian worship is not that of getting God to do something for us; it is rather expressed in the word of Jesus, "Not my will, but thine, be done." [22] This phrase is not to be interpreted in terms of abject submission, but rather in terms of freely given co-operation. It is bringing one's little life into a greater harmony with the Whole, or God.

Group worship is always performed through a ritual. Some rituals are very simple and others elaborate, some conducted in one kind of a place and some in another. A ritual is a group way of expressing or living out basic needs and insights; a means of expressing aspirations, hopes, life and faith which a group holds in common. It takes meanings which may not be too clearly perceived by all of the group and brings them out into a fuller conscious realization. The symbols of the ritual, and the various acts into which these symbols are cast, actualize something which, because of its very nature, cannot be fully comprehended nor expressed verbally. In genuine worship, not only the intellect, but also the emotional and volitional aspects of personality are engaged, stimulated and united in common purposes which are of significance, not only to the individual, but also to the group. In worship the group can also bring its negative experiences and meanings, such as feelings of guilt, into expression in a way which permits their modification. These things are not done through conscious direction or intention. Worship is an art, and like all arts its values come as one gives himself to it for its own sake and on its own terms.

The unconscious processes in our minds are of deep significance for worship. They can find expression through the symbolism of worship without the individual being aware of them. They may also be brought into the focus of conscious attention, so that the person does become aware of them through worship. At times this awareness is disturbing, and the person needs the help of a well-trained pastor to work through the problem. At other times this experience is very positive and creative, and results in personality growth.

The rituals of worship, though they have tremendous positive value, may also be used in unhealthy ways. This occurs when the ritual becomes an end in itself, when attention is focused on the symbols rather than on what the symbols are seeking to express, where meanings are divorced from the form and the form becomes of central importance. This devitalizing of worship makes it possible to go through all of the forms of worship without the realization of the meaning which these forms are seeking to express. The aspirations, hopes, love, faith, fear, guilt of the worshiper are completely repressed.

This devitalization can occur in any form of worship, from the highly elaborate to the most simple kind of ritual. No form is a guarantee against it. The crux is not in the form but in the attitude of the worshiper, and the way in which the ritual is used.

It was this problem which Jesus faced in talking with the Woman at the Well as recorded in the fourth chapter of the Gospel of John. She raised the kind of question which those who emphasize form to the neglect of inner meaning find very important. But Jesus focused the conversation on the central issue, either from the point of view of the woman's personal life or from that of worship, for one leads to the other. Does one in worship get behind the symbolic form to the inner meaning? Does the worshiper comprehend the truth which is expressed in the act and bring his life into a closer relationship to God and to his fellow men through that truth? When the ritual brings the congregation to pray, "Thy will be done," are the worshipers just saying words, or are they making individual decisions which involve the doing of God's will? When the congregation participates in a prayer of confession, are the worshipers becoming aware of that which they need to confess, and are they able to accept the conditions which make the acceptance of forgiveness possible? When a hymn of praise is sung, does a worshiper feel a genuine sense of praise and see the reasons for it; or does he seek to examine himself as to why he cannot share the mood of the hymn; or does he put on a good show of singing all the more loudly because he does not feel like praising God? This need to get beneath the symbols of worship to their meaning in our lives seems so simple that it hardly needs to be said. Yet failure to do this is the deepest weakness of worship in our churches, and a major factor in determining whether worship is a contributing factor in health or illness, as well as to salvation.

This unhealthy use of ritual is related to the compulsive use which is grounded in the strong feeling that unless one engages in a certain form at required times something undesirable will happen. One therefore conforms to the demands of the ritual in order to avoid trouble or to feel safe. It can be recognized that there is anxiety in such a situation. The person does not know why he is anxious; the reasons for the anxiety remain below the conscious level. But he feels driven to perform certain acts in definitely pre-scribed ways for the sake of finding reassurance. There is an element of magic and infantile wishful thinking here. It relieves one from the necessity of facing and resolving conflicts which are very deep and painful.

Any kind of activity can be developed into compulsive rituals. A man may run his business according to certain set and rigid proce-dures to which all his employees must conform. Order and proce-dures are important in many phases of life, but the compulsive individual overemphasizes these and makes them ends in them-selves. Some teachers insist on very formal procedures in the class-room and become disturbed if these procedures are challenged. Preachers and laymen may have similar notions about running the church, or the order of worship, or having others believe exactly as they believe.

Many people devise rituals which have no meaning to other per-sons. They have a ritual about dressing or undressing, about check-ing on the lights or the door or the stove, about their manner of eating. Such rituals grow out of specific emotional conflicts. The relation between the ritual and the conflict is usually vague and obscure, but can be discovered through the process of psycho-therapy. But the ritual serves to allay anxiety and symbolically to express and gratify a wish. The hand-washing ritual in Lady Macbeth is an attempt to deal with her murderous impulses and the guilt which they created.

Many persons make a compulsive use of religious rituals without realizing it. This has led to the charge that religion is just a mass compulsive neurosis. The charge is false though there is some basis for it, and those who have a narrow view of religion are not likely to see the other side. The crux of the situation is precisely at the point of whether the person is becoming increasingly aware of the inner feelings and relationships with which he is struggling, and whether he is able gradually to resolve the conflicts and achieve emotional and spiritual growth. Or are these feelings and relationships kept from awareness, and is there constant dependence on childish, fantastic and magical ways of dealing with the anxiety? Genuine religious experience moves toward the first alternative though there may be some of the second present also. True religious leadership is aware of the differences.

Some persons seek to allay their feelings of guilt through compulsive private and public worship experiences. They never miss a day in private devotions and are always present at public worship. If anything prevents attendance, such as a physical illness, they are very disturbed. Their religion is a constant attempt to keep their feelings of guilt out of their conscious mind and to maintain a false feeling of forgiveness. But it is a never-ending and unsatisfying process, because they are not dealing honestly with the realities of their emotional life.

A ritual can be a means of helping a person find release from guilt when it gives him sufficient strength to face the roots of his guilt, to make a confession, to relate his feelings to actual sources of guilt in his life, and to make whatever changes in attitudes and relationships may be necessary to the acceptance of forgiveness. Perhaps this cannot be done in one worship experience; it may take a longer time. Or a person may need to talk his situation over with his pastor. The central point is that the healthy use of religious ritual requires the facing of real situations in the inner life of the worshiper, changing those which need change and strengthening those which should be continued. But worship cannot be separated from the total life of the worshiper and from other aspects of religious experience, so that at times other approaches are also needed. A person who is "going to work everything out by prayer" may be one who is seeking to avoid other necessary approaches to painful experience.

This point of view may disturb those who are looking for a specific pattern of worship which will lead them to health. There is no such pattern. The sixth chapter of Isaiah is often accepted as a pattern of true worship, but many creative worship experiences have followed other patterns. Praise, adoration, gratitude, confession, affirmation of faith, the dedication of life—these occur in worship but not necessarily in the same order at all times. There should be a great deal of spontaneity in private worship, and the pattern should be determined by individual needs. The spontaneous experience of worship which may occur when one sees a sunset—whether it be adoration, awe and wonder, renewal of faith or dedication— may be of far greater value than many well-planned and carefully carried out devotional activities where no honest expression is achieved. Whatever prevents us from making a genuine response to God when such a response is evoked hurts us. The real value of any form is that it leads us to spontaneity that in turn seeks and creates new forms.

In public worship the problem of being genuine and spontaneous is somewhat different. Here we must have a ritual since a group must act together. But the ritual may be followed in utter coldness and indifference, it may be followed with artificially produced responses which give the appearance of worship but have no depth. Or we may learn how to use form to express what we feel inwardly. Form can be a means of spontaneous expression only after we have mastered it as such. It can kill spontaneous expression when we become subservient to it. The techniques of the violin may be a means of releasing the soul of the artist in great music; but one who is just a technician, not an artist, will find no release.

There is a sense in which all men worship something, even though they may not be aware of it. To worship is to give ourselves, our love, our loyalty, our devotion, our energy, to some person or object and to receive in return the fruits of that relationship. Man is so created that he either must give himself to something or turn in on himself in a deteriorating illness. But that to which he gives himself will have a controlling influence on his health and destiny. This is the insight in the temptation of Jesus in which he was offered the kingdoms of the world and the glory of them if he would worship Satan.[23] Satan certainly stands for all that is evil, harmful, destructive in human life. But men have worshiped evil, and have devoted themselves to it with great effort and ingenuity. And this has been evident in the outcome of their lives. This kind of worship can lead only to illness, disintegration and self-destruction in one form or another. But Jesus maintained his wholeness, his integrity and his undivided loyalty and devotion to God: "You shall worship the Lord your God, and him only shall you serve." A point of self-examination is the object of our real worship and devotion. Participation in Christian worship should aid in this experience.

Genuine Christian worship results in a greater capacity for relationships with God and with our fellow men on the basis of faith and love. This is not the result of magical changes or experiences in which we have no responsibility. It is the result of experiences in which we respond with love and faith to the love of God in Christ, and which leads us to deal honestly, openly and constructively with aspects of our experience which are in conflict with these responses. It is an experience in which being and becoming, not doing, are central. Being and becoming is expressed in terms of more adequate, helpful relationships with others. Worship is therefore an experience in which both persons and community grow simultaneously. Real worship brings a sense of Christian community. A sense of Christian community in turn helps its members to become more aware of their real potential—the image of God.

## The Serving Community

Service is as deeply rooted in the Christian community as are believing and worshiping. For Jesus was among men as one who served. Throughout the Gospels there is the picture of a man spending himself for others in a genuine spirit of self-giving. And at times when his disciples were absorbed with the thought of what they were going to get out of his movement he reminded them that "the Son of man also came not to be served but to serve, and to give his life as a ransom for many." [24] The worshiping church is a fellowship in which individuals find a sense of belonging and significance through ministering to the needs of others.

But like believing and worshiping, service is subject to the influence of destructive forces which distort it and make it unhealthy. At times service seems to mean just "doing good," without sufficient consideration for the reason and motivation for the doing. Some activity which passes for service may be harmful to the server and to the recipient. What are some of the factors which make service healthy or unhealthy, Christian or not Christian?

Life is a process of receiving from others, of using what we receive for our own growth, and of giving ourselves to others. We have seen earlier that the child who does not receive love and respect does not grow in a healthy manner emotionally. One aspect of unhealthy emotional growth is the inability to give of oneself in relationship with others. Health requires that we not only receive, but that we are also able to give. By giving we mean spending or investing our energy in relationships and activities which are meaningful to others. But this giving must be done with a sense of freedom and spontaneity. It is at this point of inner motivation that the difference between healthy and unhealthy aspects of service is likely to occur.

In the New Testament there is one central motivation for Christian service. This is the kind of love which out of its own richness and fullness gives of itself to meet the needs of others. The parable of the Good Samaritan [25] clearly illustrates this motivation. Two men, a priest and a Levite, saw the need, but could not give. For some reason which the story does not bring out, they were locked-up souls who probably rationalized their sickness by saying that they had more important things than this miserable, wounded person to take care of. But the Samaritan was free to feel with the suffering man, and feeling with him, having compassion, was moved to do what obviously needed to be done. However, he asked nothing in return; his service had no strings attached. Christian service gives out of a sense of gratitude for what one has received and because others need; giving is not a means of getting something in return. This kind of giving requires a high level of emotional and spiritual maturity.

This same kind of motivation is emphasized by St. Paul when in the thirteenth chapter of I Corinthians he writes, "If I give away all I have, and if I deliver my body to be burned, but have not love, I gain nothing." The giving which seeks its own gain uses others as means to an end, and destroys the finest and most needed qualities of human relationship. The giving which feels with others and therefore springs spontaneously from the giver brings with it a sense of oneness, fellowship, reconciliation. The man by the roadside needed more than his wounds bound; he needed a demonstration that there were some persons who would feel with him and help him rather than hurt him. A thousand sermons would not have told him as much as this one act. Christian service is the demonstration of the faith and worship of the Christian community.

So strong was this conviction about the central part service plays in life that Jesus made this the major emphasis in the parable of the Judgment.[26] "For I was hungry and you gave me food, I was thirsty and you gave me drink, I was a stranger and you welcomed me, I was naked and you clothed me, I was sick and you visited me, I was in prison and you came to me." And it is further very clear that within his thinking any service to the "least of these" is service to God. We serve God by serving men. But the very outcome of life, the deeper and most satisfying meanings, on the one hand, or the poverty of our existence, on the other, are dependent on our ability to feel with others and respond to their needs without thought of our own gain.

In the parable of the Talents [27] there are two men who are free to serve in the sense of taking what they were given and investing it as their Master meant it to be invested. The third man was too fearful to use what he had been given, and he rationalized his fear, that is, he made excuses defending it. But he suffers because he sought to hold what had been given him rather than to use it. To hold in this sense is to lose; to give is to grow and to become more fully our real selves.

One of the false motives for service is the desire to avoid facing our own problems. Sometimes we do this by developing a need to change others. They are wrong; we must correct them. They are sinners; we must save them from their sins. This takes our attention from ourselves, our own weaknesses, sins and errors. Psychologically this is known as projection; seeing our weaknesses in others, blaming, punishing, or trying to change them. Reforming others often springs out of a need in the reformer to avoid his own problems.

Jesus seemed acutely aware of this tendency. He cautioned men against the kind of censorious judgment which is a projection of one's own problems. He pointed out that they will be judged with the very judgment they pronounce; they are really judging and condemning themselves when they condemn others. Any sense of fellowship, and any move toward reconciliation is destroyed by this attitude. His followers should be more concerned with their own, than with the faults of others. "Why do you see the speck that is in your brother's eye, but do not notice the log that is in your own eye? Or how can you say to your brother, 'Let me take the speck out of your eye,' when there is the log in your own eye? You hypocrite, first take the log out of your own eye, and then you will see clearly to take the speck out of your brother's eye." [28] Repentance for one's own and compassion for another's weaknesses is the Christian emphasis. The desire to reform others does not fulfill the Christian spirit nor the basic conditions of health. Christian repentance has a great deal in common with what the psychologist talks about as the need to face and resolve one's own problems. Repentance is a condition of Christian service.

Jesus also met those who see service to others as a means of getting power and prestige. James and John, the sons of Zebedee, had followed and served Jesus, and felt it was time they put in their bid for their reward. And their reward was to be a position of power and prestige over the other disciples. But Jesus had no such reward to give. A man's place in the kingdom of God is to be determined, not by selfish wishes for power, but by his capacity to give himself in compassion for others. "Whoever would be great among you must be your servant, and whoever would be first among you must be slave of all." [29] The greatness of Jesus lay in his capacity to give himself completely without asking for power over others. He left men free to accept or reject him. Modern psychologists tell us that persons who seek power and prestige are motivated by anxiety and hostility, not love.[30] Sometimes these destructive feelings find expression under the guise of love.

Jesus also understood the "weary in well-doing" person, the person who works and serves overmuch and resents the fact that others do not drive themselves so hard. Martha was such a person.[31] Distracted by much serving, she finally complained to Jesus, "Do you not care that my sister has left me to serve alone? Tell her then to help me." But Jesus took a different approach. He called attention to her anxiety, and pointed to her need for ceasing from her activities, and for discovering something of the truth about herself. Mary, who had been listening to his teaching, had chosen the better part. Service which is motivated by anxiety rather than love usually leads to resentment. One feels sorry for himself, that he has to work so hard, and envious of those who do not. Activity is not the answer to emotional and spiritual problems. The answer lies in resolving the conflicts out of which the anxiety grows so that one is free to serve out of love. Martha represents a type of unhealthy activity and service which is very common today.

Jesus likewise met the person whose life was ineffective because he was trying to serve conflicting masters. He put it very plainly: "No one can serve two masters; for either he will hate the one and love the other, or he will be devoted to the one and despise the other. You cannot serve God and mammon." [32] A common emotional problem is here stated in graphic, objective terms. At times persons are caught in a conflict between their impulses and their conscience; they try to serve both and find themselves hopelessly entangled in anxiety and guilt. At times an individual feels both love and hate toward a given person and wants to express each of these feelings, though he may not be aware of his conflicting feelings. But he will feel divided, torn and guilty. At times a person's desire for power may conflict with the giving of his affection. Such conflicts will not only disturb health, but also vitiate religious experience. Motivations are consciously felt as values, as something which we want to have or to do. We objectify them, and then seek to achieve them. Conflict in motivation means conflict in values; we try to serve God and mammon because we are divided within. The result is a kind of paralysis, we stand still or vacillate but we do not grow. Indecision and doubt are often symptoms of this inner condition.

Positive Christian service, then, is not so much a matter of doing as it is of being; the meaning of our activity depends upon our motivation. Christian service is not a matter of getting power over others, but the ability to give oneself to others without thought of what they will give in return. It is only in this way that we prevent injury to the self-respect and dignity of those whom we serve, and also that we permit others to give to us. The weak are dependent on the strong, but emotionally dependent persons need the kind of relationships with others through which immature dependencies are outgrown. Service which aims at preserving dependency is unhealthy and unchristian. The mature person is able to accept realistic and legitimate dependencies on others, while at the same time being self-reliant, co-operative, and self-giving. This is essential to Christian community; for this community is not one of inferior-superior relationships, but one of brotherhood under a common Fatherhood. Giving to people with strings attached destroys any sense of Christian community. The answer to this problem is basically in the kind of persons we are; others need us more because of what we can be to them, than because of what we can do for them.

But is there not some satisfaction in the act of serving? Yes; the satisfaction which comes in the sheer joy of giving. The mature Christian is one who finds his joy in the giving itself, in the knowledge that he is able to bring something of value to another person. He holds himself in trust as something which is to be given as the needs of others require, and in this giving he allows others to become their true selves. The parent who feels joy in the giving to his children will give them freedom to become themselves and will find joy in their fulfillment. This is evidently what St. Paul had in mind when he wrote to the Corinthians that we may give our body to be burned, but without love we gain nothing. It is love which leads us to find joy in the giving itself. Satisfactions there must be in life; the question is whether the kind of satisfactions we seek are mature and creative.

But real giving of ourselves is not always free of pain. Indeed, at times it is very painful. Jesus found satisfaction in the giving of himself which was greater than his pain. At least, this is the interpretation given by the author of Hebrews, when he speaks of Jesus, "who for the joy that was set before him endured the cross, despising the shame, and is seated at the right hand of the throne of God." [33] The picture of life as constant happiness is neither mature nor Christian. The Christian finds in the Cross the insight that the complete giving of himself will require sacrifice, that suffering endured through genuine, self-giving love is redemptive, and that there is joy in fulfillment.

In the Christian faith the kind of relationship which God offers to us in Christ is one of love, of acceptance, of forgiveness, of reconciliation. It is through the realization of this love within ourselves, and through our identification with Christ, that we gain freedom to be servants of one another through love. The Christian faith is not a set of moralisms, not an external pattern of behavior, but an inner response of acceptance of God's love which leads to wholeness and to a strong desire to give to others as we have received. It was this relationship with God which made it possible for Jesus to be what he was and to give himself completely to the healing and saving of men. "Jesus, knowing that the Father had given all things into his hands, and that he had come from God and was going to God, rose from supper, laid aside his garments, and girded himself with a towel. Then he poured water into a basin, and began to wash the disciples' feet, and to wipe them with the towel with which he was girded." [34] Here the love of Christ expressed in an act of common service, creates a responsive community.

*Appendix*

# Fields for Service in the Area of Health and Religion

Since this book has grown in part out of a long experience in ministering to sick persons, it seems fitting to include an appendix in which some concrete fields of Christian service are indicated.

First, we can give money to the extent of our ability. Ministry to the ill requires large financial resources for buildings and equipment. But with our money we must also give something of ourselves. This requires an intelligent compassion for the needs of our community.

Second, some can give professionally. The need for doctors, nurses and other workers with the ill who are motivated by the spirit of Chirst is tremendous. The healing value of the best medical and nursing arts and skills is greatly enhanced by a real Christian spirit in the practitioner. Persons are being cared for here, not just sick organs. The need for medical missionaries is great, but they should be persons with a high degree of wholeness and health, as well as having a deep Christian motivation.

Third, we can study the needs of hospitals and homes for the ill and dependent in our community. We can talk with doctors, nurses, social workers, chaplains, administrators, and seek to discover the real needs of these institutions and their patients. We can discuss

157

with our friends or with a church group what can be done to meet some of these needs. We can work closely with the officials of the institutions who are in a position to give guidance, and under the guidance of doctors and nurses visit the forgotten people in these institutions, but not in order to "convert" them; just because they are persons who need an expression of Christian fellowship. The Commission on Religion and Health of the National Council of Churches, 297 Fourth Avenue, New York 10, New York, has some helpful literature, as do certain denominational agencies.

Fourth, we can study the religious work in these hospitals and discover what we can do to assist in it. There is a great need to improve the religious ministry in many church-related hospitals and in many private and state-owned hospitals. But we should remember that an adequate religious ministry in hospitals requires a kind of special training that many pastors and most laymen have not been privileged to receive. The need for adequate training for those who are to serve the ill should be emphasized, and all religious work in hospitals should be under the supervision of an adequately trained chaplain. Much harm can be done to sick persons in the name of religion.

Fifth, as a fundamental, long-range service, we can support those institutions which are giving training to pastors in this field of the ministry to the ill and in pastoral counseling. This means basically the theological schools. Many theological schools are not in a position to improve their training in this field because of lack of financial resources. Christian laymen should be aware of the fact that medical and scientific education today has access to financial resources from large foundations which will not consider theological education. Laymen who are interested in supporting religious work will find few places where their money will multiply itself in influence and service more than in institutions where leadership is being trained.

# Notes *

## CHAPTER 1

[1] Ps. 139:7.
[2] References to the healing miracles. Where the same story seems to be repeated, only one reference is given. Mark 1:40–45; Luke 17:11–19; Mark 5:25–34; John 5:1–18; Mark 8:22–26; Mark 10:46–52; John 9:1–41; Luke 13:10–17; Luke 14:1–6; Mark 1:29–31; Mark 3:1–6; Mark 5:1–20; Mark 1:23–28; Matt. 9:32–33; Mark 7:32–37; Matt. 9:1–8; Matt. 9:18–26; Mark 7:24–30; Matt. 8:5–13; Mark 9:14–29.
[3] Hos. 6:1, 2, 6.
[4] Jer. 30:17.
[5] Rev. 22:2.
[6] Gen. 1 and 2.
[7] Gen. 25:29–34.
[8] Matt. 4:1–4.
[9] I John 3:1.
[10] John 1:12.
[11] Rom. 8:14.
[12] Gal. 3:26.
[13] Gen. 1 and 2.
[14] I Cor. 3:16, 17.
[15] Luke 12:1–3.
[16] Luke 6:45.
[17] Eph. 3:16.
[18] Gal. 5:13–25.
[19] Matt. 4:1.
[20] Gal. 6:7.
[21] Matt. 6:22, 23.

## CHAPTER 2

[1] Bonaro Overstreet, *Understanding Fear in Ourselves and Others* (New York: Harper & Brothers, 1951).
[2] Paul Tillich, *The Courage to Be* (New Haven: Yale University Press, 1952). Our very brief summary here fails to do justice to Dr. Tillich's thought. The book must be read to get this in its fullness.
[3] Ps. 111:10; Matt. 6:25; Matt. 10:26–31; Luke 10:41; Phil. 4:6; I John 4:18.

* Scriptural quotations are from the Revised Standard Version.

⁴ Ps. 23:1; Mark 5:34; Heb. 11:1.
⁵ Gen. 3:1–24.
⁶ Gen. 25:29–34.
⁷ Luke 10:38–42.
⁸ Ps. 111:10; see also Job 28:28.
⁹ Heb. 12:28.
¹⁰ II Tim. 1:7.
¹¹ I John 4:18.
¹² Matt. 10:16–33.
¹³ See Pss. 23, 103, 91, 46, 34, 90.
¹⁴ Matt. 6:19–34.
¹⁵ Matt. 4:1–11.
¹⁶ Matt. 26:36–46; Luke 22:39–46.
¹⁷ Phil. 4:6.
¹⁸ Isa. 26:3.
¹⁹ Heb. 11:1.
²⁰ Matt. 9:22; Mark 5:34; Luke 8:48.
²¹ John 4:46–53; Matt. 8:5–13; Matt. 9:18–26.
²² II Cor. 12:7.
²³ Eph. 2:8.

## CHAPTER 3

¹ Mark 2:1–12.
² Gen. 4:1–16.
³ Gen. 37.
⁴ Matt. 5:17–20.
⁵ Luke 15:11–32.
⁶ Luke 19:1–10.
⁷ Luke 22:31–34; 54–62.
⁸ Luke 22:3–6; 47–53.
⁹ John 8:1–11; see also Mark 2:15–17; Luke 15:1–10; John 3:17.
¹⁰ Matt. 18:23–35; Matt. 6:12.
¹¹ Matt. 7:1.
¹² Matt. 7:24–27; Matt. 25:1–13; Luke 12:16–21.
¹³ Mark 3:29; Matt. 12:31; 32; Luke 12:10.
¹⁴ Luke 13:1–3.
¹⁵ Luke 13:4, 5.
¹⁶ John 9:1–12.
¹⁷ Matt. 18:22.
¹⁸ Matt. 6:12; 18:21–35.
¹⁹ II Cor. 5:19.
²⁰ Rom. 5:8.
²¹ Rom. 5:20.
²² James 5:16; I John 1:9.
²³ Matt. 3:2; Mark 1:15, 6:12; Rom. 2:4.

## CHAPTER 4

¹ Matt. 22:37–40.
² Sigmund Freud, *Collected Papers*, Vol. IV, London, Hogarth Press, 1924, p. 42.

³ Eric Fromm, *Psychoanalysis and Religion,* New Haven, Yale University Press, 1950, p. 87.
⁴ Gen. 4:1‐16.
⁵ Luke 15:11–32.
⁶ Gen., chaps. 37–50.
⁷ Exod. 20:13.
⁸ Prov. 6:16.
⁹ Ps. 90:7.
¹⁰ Ps. 38:3.
¹¹ Amos 5:15.
¹² Mic. 3:2.
¹³ Matt. 5:21–26.
¹⁴ Matt. 5:38–42.
¹⁵ Matt. 5:43–48.
¹⁶ Luke 6:22; John 3:20; John 15:18; Luke 15:28.
¹⁷ Acts 7:54–8:3; Acts 9:1–30.
¹⁸ Rom. 7:15.
¹⁹ Luke 6:37–38.
²⁰ Luke 7:36–50.
²¹ Eph. 2:14.
²² Mark 1:11.
²³ Matt. 17:5.
²⁴ Luke 11:2.
²⁵ Matt. 10:32.
²⁶ Matt. 25:34.
²⁷ Matt. 11:25–30.
²⁸ Mark 14:36.
²⁹ Luke 23:34.
³⁰ Luke 23:46.
³¹ Luke 19:1–10; John 3:1–15; John 4:1–30; John 8:1–11; Matt. 26:30–35, 26:69–75; Acts 2, 3; Matt. 26:21–25, 47–56.
³² John 1:1, 14.
³³ John 3:16.
³⁴ I John 4:7–12, 18, 19.
³⁵ Luke 15:11–32.
³⁶ Matt. 25:1–13.
³⁷ Matt. 25:14–30.
³⁸ Matt. 25:31–46.
³⁹ Matt. 22:37–40.
⁴⁰ John 13:34, 35.
⁴¹ John 15:12, 13.
⁴² Matt. 27; Mark 15; Luke 23; John 19.
⁴³ Mark 15:34.
⁴⁴ Luke 23:46.
⁴⁵ Eph. 4:32.

## CHAPTER 5

¹ For a fuller discussion of the Christian Community from the Biblical point of view see a forthcoming book by Dr. Otto J. Baab.
² Luke 19:1–10.

[3] John 4:1–30.
[4] John 8:1–11.
[5] Mark 2:1–12.
[6] Phil. 2:1, 2.
[7] Phil. 1:5.
[8] II Cor. 13:14.
[9] Rom. 12:5.
[10] I Cor. 12:27.
[11] I John 1:3.
[12] John 15.
[13] John 13:34, 35.
[14] John 17:20–21.
[15] James 5:16; I John 1:9.
[16] Matt. 9:1–17; 12:1–13.
[17] John 1:12.
[18] John 9.
[19] Matt. 25:14–46.
[20] Eph. 2:19.
[21] Matt. 5:23; see also the discussion of this passage in chap. 4.
[22] Luke 22:42.
[23] Matt. 4:8–11.
[24] Mark 10:45.
[25] Luke 10:25–37.
[26] Matt. 25:31–46; see also the discussion of this parable in chap. 4.
[27] Matt. 25:14–30; see also the discussion of this parable in chap. 4.
[28] Matt. 7:1–5.
[29] Mark 10:32–45.
[30] For further reading on this theme see Karen Horney, *Neuroses and Human Growth* (New York: W. W. Norton Co., 1950).
[31] Luke 10:38–42; see also the discussion of this story in chap. 2.
[32] Matt. 6:24.
[33] Heb. 12:2.
[34] John 13:3–5.

# Books for Further Reading

Blair, Edward P. *The Bible and You*. Nashville and New York, Abingdon Press, 1953. A discussion of methods of Bible study written for the layman.

English, O. Spurgeon, and Pearson, Gerald H. J. *Emotional Problems of Living*. New York, W. W. Norton Co., 1945. A volume which covers the development of personality from infancy to old age, emphasizing the emotional problems which arise at different levels of growth. The point of view is psychoanalytic; style is nontechnical and easy to read.

Goodenough, Erwin R. *Toward a Mature Faith*. New York, Prentice-Hall, Inc., 1955. One man's account of his religious growth related to the psychological understanding of man. Rewarding reading.

Howe, Reuel. *Man's Need and God's Action*. Greenwich, Conn., Seabury Press, 1953. A very helpful discussion of the relation of certain aspects of Christian experience to emotional problems and conditions.

May, Rollo. *The Meaning of Anxiety*. New York, The Ronald Press, 1950. The most comprehensive work on anxiety; scholarly, requiring some background in psychology and philosophy.

Maves, Paul (ed.). *The Church and Mental Health*. New York, Charles Scribner's Sons, 1954. A symposium dealing with various problems in relation of religion to mental health. Of particular value to the pastor.

Neill, William. *The Rediscovery of the Bible*. New York, Harper & Brothers, 1955. Deals with the result of Biblical scholarship over the last half century, and with the value of the Bible today.

Overstreet, Bonaro W. *Understanding Fear in Ourselves and Others*. New York, Harper & Brothers, 1951. A helpful discussion of fear, utilizing psychological and religious insights.

Phillips, J. B. *Making Men Whole*. New York, The Macmillan Company, 1953. A stimulating book by an English clergyman and Biblical scholar who has some appreciation of the psychological aspects of religious experience.

Richardson, Alan. *A Theological Word Book of the Bible*. New York,

164    *Psychiatry* and the Bible

The Macmillan Company, 1951. A scholarly work of particular value
to the pastor, but would be helpful to laymen who have done wide
study in the field. Very helpful in illuminating the meaning of theological words as found in the Bible. Condenses much Biblical
scholarship.

Roberts, David E. *Psychotherapy and a Christian View of Man*. New
York, Charles Scribner's Sons, 1950. A professor of theology discusses
theological concepts of man in relation to psychological concepts of
man. A very helpful book for the reader with some background.

Tillich, Paul. *The Courage to Be*. New Haven, Conn., Yale University
Press, 1952. A philosophical discussion of anxiety, the threat of non-
being, in relation to a religious faith which takes anxiety into itself
and thus overcomes it. Difficult reading but rewarding.

Tillich, Paul. *The New Being*. New York, Charles Scribner's Sons,
1955. A book of sermons which deal with various personal situations
with sound theological and psychological insights.

Wise, Carroll A. *Religion in Illness and Health*. New York, Harper &
Brothers, 1942. A study of religious factors in mental illness and
health with emphasis on the use of religious symbols in fostering and
formulating inner meanings which lead to these conditions.

——. *Pastoral Counseling, Its Theory and Practice*. New York,
Harper & Brothers, 1951. An interpretation of the theory and practice
of pastoral counseling, primarily for pastors, but would help laymen
understand the place of this service within the Church.

# TOPICAL INDEX

165

# SCRIPTURE INDEX

167

Date Due